Air Fryer

150 Delicious, Quick And Easy To Make Air Fryer Recipes Cookbook You And Your Family Will Absolutely Love

by
Annabel Bay

Table Of Content

Introduction

The world nowadays is developing at a really fast pace and every few days we witness the
Invention of a new gadget and one of those few gadgets is the Airfryer.

A new gadget that saves you a lot of money that you usually spend on oil as well as protect your body from many diseases caused by junk food and fried foods that holds in them so many cholesterol which is known for being responsible of so many deadly diseases such as obesity, blood pressure, cancer...

Using an airfry will make your life so much easier at is enable you to prepare some very easy tasty recipes in a matter of minutes without having to put too much work in them.

If you just purchased, already own or you think about purchasing an Airfryer but you have no idea what and how to cook in it; this book offers you 150 easy tasty recipes with simple ingredients and explicit directions on how to make them.

From fries to steaks, rolls, burgers, cakes, muffins to cupcakes...an Airfryer can cook anything you put in it perfectly and the best thing about it is that it doesn't need you constant attention, all you have to do is to set the timer and it will cook your meal perfectly for you.

So put on you apron, and let's get that Airfryer to work!!!!

Rosemary Chips

Serves: 2
Prep Time: 45 min
Ingredients:

- 4 medium russet potatoes, thinly sliced
- 1 tablespoon of olive oil
- 2 teaspoon of fresh rosemary, finely chopped
- Black pepper
- Salt

Directions:

1. Preheat the Airfryer on 330 F for 3 min.
2. Soak the potato slices in a salted pot of water for 30 min.
3. Once the time is up, drain the potato slices and pat them dry.
4. Toss the potato slices in a large bowl with the rosemary, olive oil and a pinch of salt in a large bowl then airfry them for 30 min while shaking them every once in a while.
5. Serve your chips and enjoy.

Fried Salmon Croquettes

Serves: 16
Prep Time: 12 min
Ingredients:

- 1 pound of canned red salmon, drained
- 3.5 ounces of bread crumbs
- 1/3 cup of vegetable oil
- ½ bunch of parsley, roughly chopped
- 2 egg, beaten
- Black pepper
- Salt

Directions:

1. Preheat the Airfryer on 400 F for 5 min.
2. Mix the oil with breadcrumbs in a small bowl then set it aside.
3. Combine the remaining ingredients in another mixing bowl and mash them slightly with a fork then shape the mix into 16 balls.
4. Roll the salmon croquettes in the breadcrumbs mix then airfry them in batches for 7 min for each batch.
5. Serve your salmon croquettes warm and enjoy.

Classic Brussels Sprouts

Serves: 4
Prep Time: 35 min
Ingredients:
- 1 pound of fresh Brussels sprouts
- 1 ½ tablespoon of olive oil
- Salt

Directions:

1. Preheat the Airfryer on 400 for 5 min.
2. Toss the Brussels sprouts in a large bowl with the olive oil and a pinch of salt.
3. Transfer them to the airfry then Airfry them for 25.
4. Once the time is up, serve your Brussels sprouts warm and enjoy.

Onion Rings

Serves: 1 to 2
Prep Time: 25 min
Ingredients:
- 1 large white onion, sliced into ¼ inch rings
- 1 ¼ cup of purpose flour
- 1 cup of milk
- 1 egg
- ¾ cup of bread crumbs
- 1 teaspoon of baking powder
- 1 teaspoon of Salt

Directions:

1. Preheat the Airfryer on 360 for 10 min.
2. Whisk the eggs with milk in a small bowl then set it aside.
3. Mix the flour with baking powder and salt in another bowl and set it aside.
4. Dust the onion rings in the flour mix then dip them in the egg and milk mix and roll them in the breadcrumbs.
5. Place the onion rings in the Airfryer and airfry them for 7 to 10 min then serve them and enjoy.

Airfried Ravioli

Serves: 2 to 4
Prep Time: 12 min
Ingredients:

- 1 box of your favorite ravioli
- 2 cups of breadcrumbs
- 1 cup of buttermilk
- ¼ cup of parmesan cheese, grated
- Black pepper
- Salt

Directions:

1. Preheat the Airfryer on 200 F for 3 min.
2. Season the breadcrumbs with a pinch of salt and pepper then mix it with the parmesan cheese in a small bowl.
3. Dip the raw ravioli in the buttermilk then coat it with the breadcrumbs.
4. Place the ravioli in the Airfryer and airfry it for 5 min.
5. Once the time is up, serve your ravioli warm with some marinara sauce and enjoy.

Crispy Pickles

Serves: 4
Prep Time: 20 min
Ingredients:

- 12 ounces of dill pickles slices, drained
- 2/3 cup of purpose flour
- 1/3 cup of yellow corn meal
- 2 teaspoons of garlic powder
- 2 teaspoons of paprika
- 1 teaspoon of cayenne pepper
- Salt

Directions:

1. Preheat the Airfryer on 390 F for 3 min.
2. Drain the pickles and pat them dry.
3. Mix the remaining ingredients in a mixing bowl then add in the pickles and toss them.
4. Airfry the pickles on 3 batches for 4 to 6 min then serve them and enjoy.

Crusty Mushroom Bites

Serves: 10
Prep Time: 20 min
Ingredients:
- 10 button mushrooms
- 2 ounces of parmesan cheese, grated
- 3 cream crackers squares
- 1 egg white
- 1/8 teaspoon of Italian seasoning
- Black pepper
- Salt

Directions:

1. Preheat the Airfryer on 356 F for 3 min.
2. Blend the cream crackers in a food processor until it become crumbly.
3. Mix the crumbled crackers with Italian seasoning, a pinch of salt and pepper.
4. Toss the mushroom in a mixing bowl with the egg white, a pinch of salt and pepper then toss it with the crumbled crackers mix.
5. Airfry the mushroom for 14 to 16 min then serve it warm and enjoy.

Kraft Spinach Bites

Serves: 2 to 4
Prep Time: 16 min
Ingredients:

- 1 package of fresh spinach, roughly chopped
- 1 large carrot, grated
- 2 slices of kart singles cheese, diced
- 1 egg
- ½ medium yellow onion, finely chopped
- 1 tablespoon of corn flour
- 1 teaspoon of garlic, minced
- ½ teaspoon of garlic powder
- Black pepper
- Salt

Directions:

1. Preheat the Airfryer on 356 F for 3 min.
2. Combine all the ingredients in large bowl and shape them into medium size balls.
3. Roll the spinach balls in some breadcrumbs then airfry them for 10 to 12 min.
4. Once the time is up, serve your spinach bites and enjoy.

Airfried Mushroom

Serves: 2 to 4
Prep Time: 35 min
Ingredients:

- 1 pound of mushroom, quartered
- 2 tablespoons of olive oil
- 1 tablespoon of duck fat
- 2 teaspoons of herbs de province
- ½ teaspoon of garlic powder
- Salt

Directions:

1. Preheat the Airfryer on 365 for 5 min.
2. Melt the duck fat in a large pan and sauté in it the garlic for 2 min then add in the remaining ingredients.
3. Transfer the mix to an Airfryer and Airfry it for 25 min.
4. Once the time is up, serve your mushroom and enjoy.

Calamari Rings

Serves: 6
Prep Time: 45 min
Ingredients:

- 1 ½ pound of baby squid, cleaned and sliced
- ½ cup of semolina flour
- ½ cup of purpose flour
- 1/3 cup of cornmeal
- 2 tablespoons of vegetable oil
- ½ teaspoon of old bay seasoning
- Black pepper
- Salt

Directions:

1. Preheat the Airfryer on 375 for 5 min.
2. Squeeze the sliced baby squid gently from the excess water and set it aside.
3. Mix the remaining ingredients in a mixing bowl then toss in them the baby squid rings.
4. Spray the airfry basket with a cooking spray then place in it 1/3 of the baby squid rings and airfry them for 10 to 12 min or until they are done.
5. Repeat the process with the 2 remaining batches then serve your calamari rings with some fresh lemon juice and enjoy.

Crunchy Sausage Croquettes

Serves: 4
Prep Time: 25 min
Ingredients:

- 3.5 ounces of sausages, casing removed
- ½ small yellow onion, diced
- 3 tablespoons of breadcrumbs
- 1 teaspoon of dry sage
- ½ teaspoon of garlic, minced
- Black pepper
- Salt

Directions:

1. Preheat the Airfryer on 356 for 5 min.
2. Mix the onion with sage, garlic and sausages in a mixing bowl then shape them into small size balls and roll them in the breadcrumbs.
3. Place the croquettes in the airfry basket and fry them for 15 min then serve them and enjoy.

Tofu Dices

Serves: 4
Prep Time: 20 min
Ingredients:

- 1 block of firm tofu, diced
- ¼ cup of parmesan cheese, grated
- ¼ cup of cornmeal
- 2 tablespoons of olive oil
- 2 tablespoons of cornstarch

Directions:

1. Preheat the Airfryer on 365 for 5 min.
2. Mix the cornmeal with cheese and cornstarch in a small bowl.
3. Coat the tofu mix with the cheese mix then place them in the Airfryer basket and drizzle the olive oil all over them.
4. Airfry the tofu for 7 min then serve them and enjoy.

Crunchy Donut Bites

Serves: 4 to 6
Prep Time: 20 min
Ingredients:

- 1 can of biscuit dough
- 1 cup of caster sugar
- 1 teaspoon of vanilla extract
- 1 teaspoon of cinnamon powder

Directions:

1. Mix the sugar with vanilla extract and cinnamon in a large bowl then set it aside.
2. Cut the biscuit dough into ¼ pieces then airfry them for 6 to 8 min.
3. Once the time is up, toss the donut bites in the caster sugar mix then serve them and enjoy.

Fish Shop Fillets

Serves: 4
Prep Time: 25 min
Ingredients:

- 14 ounces of firm white fish fillets, cut into thick strips
- 14 ounces of panko breadcrumbs
- 4 eggs
- 2 tablespoons of fresh parsley, finely chopped
- Black pepper
- Salt

Directions:

1. Preheat the Airfryer on 400 for 5 min.
2. Whisk the eggs in a small bowl then set it aside.
3. Mix the breadcrumbs with parsley and set them aside.
4. Season the fish strips with a pinch of salt and pepper then dip them in the eggs and coat them with the breadcrumbs mix.
5. Airfry the fish strips for 14 to 15 min then serve them warm and enjoy.

Crunchy Veggies Twisters

Serves: 2 to 4
Prep Time: 35 min
Ingredients:

- 1 medium sweet potato, peeled and shaved into stripes
- 2 parsnips, peeled and shaved into stripes
- 2 beetroots, peeled and shaved into stripes
- 1 tablespoon of olive oil
- ½ teaspoon of dry herbs de province
- Black pepper
- Salt

Directions:

1. Preheat the Airfryer on 400 F for 5 min.
2. Toss all the ingredients in a large bowl with a pinch of salt and pepper.
3. Place the veggies mix in the Airfryer and airfry them for 20 min then serve them and enjoy.

Crunchy French Fries

Serves: 4
Prep Time: 25 min
Ingredients:
- 2 pounds of potato, peeled and cut into sticks
- 1 tablespoons of olive oil
- Salt

Directions:

1. Preheat the Airfryer on 356 for 5 min.
2. Toss the potato with a pinch of salt and olive oil in a large bowl then airfry it for 15 min.
3. Serve your fries warm and enjoy.

Crunchy Rice Bites

Serves: 8 to 10
Prep Time: 25 min
Ingredients:

- 1 cup of white rice, cooked
- 1 cup of mozzarella, shredded
- 10 small Cheddar cheese dices
- 4 tablespoons of cold water
- 2 tablespoons of sweet corns kernels
- 2 tablespoons of fresh carrot, grated
- 1 tablespoon of corn flour
- ½ teaspoon of garlic powder
- ¼ teaspoon of Italian seasoning
- Breadcrumbs
- Black pepper
- Salt

Directions:

1. Preheat the Airfryer on 400 F for 3 min.
2. Whisk the water with corn flour in a small bowl.
3. Mix the mozzarella cheese with rice and corn flour mix, garlic powder, Italian seasoning, a pinch of salt and pepper.
4. Toss the corn kernels with carrot and cheddar cheese in a small bowl to make the filling.
5. Flatten 1 tablespoon of the rice mix in your hands then place in the middle of it some of the filling and wrap it around it gently.
6. Repeat the process with the remaining ingredients then coat the rice bites with some breadcrumbs.
7. Airfry the breadcrumbs for 12 to 16 min then serve it warm and enjoy.

Roasted Squash

Serves: 4
Prep Time: 25 min
Ingredients:

- 1 medium butternut squash, peeled and cut into chunks
- 1 tablespoon of olive oil
- 2 teaspoons of cumin seeds
- Black pepper
- Salt

Directions:

1. Preheat the Airfryer on 375 F for 5 min.
2. Toss all the ingredients in a large bowl then roast them in the Airfryer for 20 min while turning them every 10 min.
3. Once the time is up, serve your roasted butternut squash and enjoy.

Crispy Potato Wedges

Serves: 6
Prep Time: 30 min
Ingredients:

- 2 pounds of potato, cut into wedges
- 2 ½ tablespoons of olive oil
- 2 ½ teaspoons of smoked paprika
- Black pepper
- Salt

Directions:

1. Preheat the Airfryer on 356 F for 5 min.
2. Peel the potatoes and cut them into wedges then soak them in some salted water for 30 min.
3. Drain the potato wedges and pat them dry.
4. Toss the potato wedges in a large bowl with the olive oil, paprika, a pinch of salt and pepper then airfry them for 20 min.
5. Serve your potato wedges warm and enjoy.

Roasted Baby Carrots

Serves: 4 to 6
Prep Time: 30 min
Ingredients:
- 1 1/3 pounds of baby carrots
- 1 tablespoon of olive oil
- 1 teaspoon of cumin seeds
- Black pepper
- Salt

Directions:

1. Preheat the Airfryer on 400 F for 5 min.
2. Toss all the ingredients in a large bowl with a pinch of salt and pepper.
3. Airfry the carrots for 20 min then serve them warm and enjoy.

Cheesy Ham Wheels

Serves: 6
Prep Time: 15 min
Ingredients:

- 1 sheet of puff pastry
- 4 handfuls of gruyere cheese, grated
- 8 slices of ham
- 1 teaspoon of Dijon mustard
- Black pepper
- Salt

Directions:

1. Preheat the Airfryer on 370 F for 5 min.
2. Lay the sheet of puff pastry on a floured surface and spread on it the Dijon mustard then lay on them the grated cheese followed by the ham slices.
3. Roll the dough gently then wrap it tightly in a cling film and freeze it for 30 min.
4. Cut the rolled stuffed dough into ½ inches thick round the airfry them for 10 to 12 min until they become golden then serve them and enjoy.

Chicken Mozzarella Sticks

Serves: 6
Prep Time: 20 min
Ingredients:
- 1 pound of lean chicken, minced
- 6 mozzarella sticks
- 2 eggs, lightly beaten
- 1 cup of purpose flour
- 1 cup of bread crumbs
- ½ teaspoon of dry oregano
- ½ teaspoon of garlic powder
- ¼ teaspoon of onion powder
- 1/8 teaspoon of cayenne pepper
- Black pepper
- Salt

Directions:

1. Preheat the Airfryer on 356 F for 3 min.
2. Mix the chicken with cayenne pepper, garlic powder and oregano, onion powder, a pinch of salt and pepper in a large bowl.
3. Dust 1 mozzarella stick with flour then dip it in the beaten egg, cover it completely gently with the lean chicken mix then roll it in the breadcrumbs.
4. Repeat the process with the remaining mozzarella sticks.
5. Airfry the chicken mozzarella sticks for 10 to 14 min until they become golden brown they serve them warm and enjoy.

Pigs In Blankets

Serves: 8
Prep Time: 15 min
Ingredients:
- 8 chipolatas sausages
- 4 bacon fillets
- Black pepper
- Salt

Directions:

1. Preheat the Airfryer on 356 F for 5 min.
2. Cut each bacon fillet in half and wrap them around the sausages then airfry them for 10 min.
3. Serve your pig in blankets warm and enjoy.

Stuffed Potato Rolls

Serves: 8
Prep Time: 30 min
Ingredients:

- 5 large potatoes, cooked and mashed
- 8 slices of bread
- 2 small yellow onions, finely chopped
- 2 green chilies, seeded and finely chopped
- 1 small bunch of coriander, finely chopped
- 2 tablespoons of vegetable oil
- ½ teaspoon of mustard seeds
- ½ teaspoon of turmeric
- Black pepper
- Salt

Directions:

1. Preheat the Airfryer on 400 F for 10 min.
2. Heat 1 teaspoon of oil in a large pan and sauté in it the onion with mustard for 3 min then add in the potato with turmeric and turn off the heat.
3. Trim the crusty sides of a slice of bread and soak in it some water gently then drain it and press it in your hands to get rid of the excess water.
4. Divide the potato mix into 8 portions then place a portion of it on the bread in your hand and gently cover it with it.
5. Once the potato is completely covered with bread set it aside and repeat the process with the remaining ingredients.
6. Airfry the potato rolls for 12 to 15 min then serve them warm and enjoy.

Chilly Marinated Fries

Serves: 2
Prep Time: 35 min
Ingredients:
- 1 pound of potato, cut into wedges
- 2 teaspoons of chili flakes
- 1 teaspoon of cumin
- ½ teaspoon of turmeric powder
- Salt

Directions:

1. Preheat the Airfryer on 365 F for 3 min.
2. Toss all the ingredients in a large bowl then refrigerate them for 10 to 20 min.
3. Airfry the potato wedges for 15 min then serve them warm and enjoy.

Cheesy Potato Bites

Serves: 12
Prep Time: 20 min
Ingredients:

- 3 large potatoes, cooked and mashed
- 2/3 cup of breadcrumbs
- 12 mozzarella cheese small dices
- 1 teaspoon of turmeric
- ½ teaspoon of cumin
- ½ teaspoon of chili pepper flakes
- Black pepper
- Salt

Directions:

1. Preheat the Airfryer on 400 F for 5 min.
2. Mix the mashed potato with cumin, chili flakes, turmeric, a pinch of salt and pepper in a large bowl to roll them in 12 balls.
3. Flatten a potato ball in the palm of your hand gently and place a mozzarella cube inside it then wrap it around gently.
4. Repeat the process with the remaining ingredients then roll the potato bites gently in the breadcrumbs.
5. Airfry the cheesy potato bites for 10 min then serve them and enjoy.

Chickpea Fritters

Serves: 6
Prep Time: 20 min
Ingredients:

- 1 zucchini, julienned
- 1small onion, julienned
- 2/3 cup of chickpea flour
- 1 teaspoon of chili powder
- ½ teaspoon of turmeric
- Water
- Black pepper
- Salt

Directions:

1. Preheat the Airfryer on 400 F for 3 min.
2. Combine the chickpea flour with turmeric, chili powder, a pinch of and pepper in a large mixing bowl then add to them water until you get a thick batter.
3. Stir in the zucchini with onion then form them into small circles then place them in a small lineup Airfryer.
4. Airfry the fritters for 10 min then serve them and enjoy.

Stuffed Fried Okra

Serves: 4
Prep Time: 25 min
Ingredients:
- 1 pound of medium size okra, seeded
- ¼ cup of turkey, minced and cooked
- 1 yellow onion, finely chopped
- 4 tablespoons of chickpea flour
- 2 tablespoons of fresh coconut, grated
- 1 teaspoon of garam masala
- ½ teaspoon of cumin
- ½ teaspoon of turmeric
- ½ teaspoon of red chili pepper
- Black pepper
- Salt

Directions:

1. Preheat the Airfryer on 365 F for 3 min.
2. Clean the okra and seed it then set it aside.
3. Mix the remaining ingredients in a large bowl with a pinch of salt and pepper to make the filling.
4. Gently stuff the okra with the filling then brush them with some vegetable oil and airfry it for 12 min.
5. Serve your stuffed okra warm and enjoy.

Banana Split

Serves: 8
Prep Time: 20 min
Ingredients:

- 8 ripe bananas, cut into 2
- 3 egg whites
- 1 cup of panko bread crumbs
- ½ cup of corn flour
- 3 tablespoons of butter
- 3 tablespoons of cinnamon sugar

Directions:

1. Preheat the Airfryer on 280 F for 3 min.
2. Melt the butter in a pan then stir in the breadcrumbs and cook it for 3 to 4 min or until it becomes golden brown.
3. Place the breadcrumbs in a plate and allow it to cool down completely.
4. Dust the banana halves in the corn flour then dip them in the egg whites and roll them in the breadcrumbs.
5. Place the banana halves in the Airfryer basket and sprinkle the cinnamon sugar all over them then airfry them for 10 min.
6. Once the time is up, serve your bananas with your favorite ice cream and enjoy.

Crispy Green Beans

Serves: 4 to 6
Prep Time: 20 min
Ingredients:

- 2 pounds of fresh green beans, trimmed
- 2 cup of bread crumbs
- 1 cup of flour
- ½ cup of heavy cream
- 1 egg
- 2 teaspoons of paprika
- 2 teaspoons of garlic powder
- 1 teaspoon of onion powder
- Black pepper
- Salt

Directions:

1. Preheat the Airfryer on 356 F for 3 min.
2. Whisk the egg with heavy cream.
3. Mix the flour with onion powder, paprika and garlic powder.
4. Dust the green beans in the flour mix then dip them in the cream egg mix and roll them in the breadcrumbs.
5. Airfry the green beans for 6 to 10 min then serve it and enjoy.

Apple Pie Fries

Serves: 4
Prep Time: 45 min
Ingredients:

- 2 store bought pie crusts
- 10 ounces of apple pie filling
- 1 egg, beaten
- ¼ cup of caster sugar
- 1 teaspoon of cinnamon
- ¼ teaspoon of nutmeg powder

Directions:

1. Preheat the Airfryer on 356 F for 3 min.
2. Roll the pie crusts on a floured surface.
3. Pour the apple pie filling in a food processor and blend them smooth to make the filling.
4. Spread the filling all over 1 pie crust then cover it gently with the other.
5. Cut the pie into medium sized strips.
6. Mix the cinnamon with sugar and nutmeg powder in a small bowl.
7. Brush the pie strips with the beaten egg and sprinkle on them the sugar and cinnamon mix.
8. Transfer the strips into a lined up baking sheet that fits in your Airfryer then airfry them for 15 to 20 min or until they become golden brown.
9. Serve your apple pie strips with some ice cream and enjoy.

Caramelized Crunchy Nuts

Serves: 3 to 6
Prep Time: 30 min
Ingredients:

- 1 ½ cup of cashews
- 1 ½ cup of almonds
- ¼ cup of caster sugar
- 1 egg white, beaten
- 1 teaspoon of salt
- ½ teaspoon of cinnamon
- ¼ teaspoon of ground cloves

Directions:

1. Preheat the Airfryer on 300 F for 5 min and grease with a cooking spray.
2. Toss all the ingredients in a mixing bowl then pour them in the airfry and cook them for 25 min.
3. Once the time is up, allow the nuts to cool down completely then serve them warm and enjoy.

Crunchy French Sticks

Serves: 2
Prep Time: 15 min
Ingredients:
- 4 slices of bread
- 2 tablespoons of soft butter
- 2 eggs, lightly beaten
- ½ teaspoon of cinnamon powder
- ¼ teaspoon of nutmeg powder

Directions:

1. Preheat the Airfryer on 356 F for 5 min.
2. Beat the eggs lightly in a small bowl with the cinnamon, nutmeg powder and a pinch of salt.
3. Spread the butter on both bread slices then cut them into strips.
4. Dip the bread strips in the beaten egg
5. Airfry the bread strips for 2 min the flip them and cook them for another 4 min.
6. Once the time is up, sprinkle some icing sugar on the bread strips then serve them and enjoy.

Chicken Bites

Serves: 30 to 32
Prep Time: 40 min
Ingredients:

- 1 pound of chicken breast
- 8 corn tortillas
- 2 tablespoons of olive oil
- The juice of 2 limes
- 2 tablespoons of parsley, finely chopped
- 1 teaspoon of chili pepper
- Black pepper
- Salt

Directions:

1. Preheat the Airfryer on 400 F for 5 min.
2. Bring a salted pot of water to a boil then place in it the chicken and bring it to another boil.
3. Turn off the heat and allow the chicken to sit for 20 min then drain it and shred it.
4. Cut the corn tortillas and small circles with a cookie cutter then airfry them in batches for 5 min until they become crispy.
5. In the meantime, toss the shredded chicken with the remaining ingredients in a large bowl then season them with a pinch of salt and pepper.
6. Top the crunchy tortilla circles with the shredded chicken and some crumbled cheese or mango salad then serve them and enjoy.

Crunchy Tropical Shrimp

Serves: 2 to 4
Prep Time: 20 min
Ingredients:

- 1 pound of large shrimp
- ½ cup of plain flour
- 2 egg whites, lightly beaten
- ½ cup of coconut, shredded
- ½ breadcrumbs
- The zest of 1 lime
- Black pepper
- Salt

Directions:

1. Preheat the Airfryer on 400 F for 3 min.
2. Mix the lime zest with coconut and breadcrumbs in a small bowl then set it aside.
3. Season the shrimp with a pinch of salt and pepper then dust with flour.
4. Dip the shrimp in the egg white then coat with the coconut and breadcrumbs mix.
5. Airfry the shrimp for 5 to 6 min then serve it warm and enjoy.

Cheesy Buttermilk Biscuits

Serves: 8
Prep Time: 30 min
Ingredients:

- 2 1/3 cup of self raising flour
- 1 1/3 cup of buttermilk
- ½ cup of cheddar cheese, grated
- ½ cup of butter, frozen and grated
- 2 tablespoons of sugar
- 1 tablespoon of butter, melted
- Salt

Directions:

1. Preheat the Airfryer on 380 F for 3 min.
2. Combine the sugar with flour in a large mixing bowl then add in the grated butter with cheese and a pinch of salt.
3. Stir in the buttermilk until you get a smooth dough and no lumps are found.
4. Shape the dough into 8 balls then place them on a floured surface.
5. Lined up a baking pan with parchment paper and grease it then place in it the dough balls side by side.
6. Transfer the parchment paper with the dough balls gently to the Airfryer basket.
7. Brush the cheesy buttermilk balls with the melted butter and airfry them for 20 min then serve them warm and enjoy.

Garlicky Tomato Tostadas

Serves: 16 to 20
Prep Time: 25 min
Ingredients:

- 4 ripe tomatoes, sliced
- 1 tablespoon of olive oil
- 1 clove of garlic
- ½ teaspoon of dry thyme
- Salt

Directions:

1. Preheat the Airfryer on 390 F.
2. Toss all the ingredients in a large bowl with a pinch of salt then place them in the Airfryer basket and airfry them for 15 min.
3. Once the time is up, serve your Airfried tomato with some toasted bread slices and enjoy.

Roasted Cauliflower Bites

Serves: 2
Prep Time: 20 min
Ingredients:

- 17.5 ounces of broccoli florets
- 2 tablespoons of plain yogurt
- 1 tablespoon of chickpea flour
- ½ teaspoon of red chili powder
- ¼ teaspoon of turmeric
- Salt

Directions:

1. Preheat the Airfryer on 400 F for 5 min.
2. Season the broccoli with a pinch of salt and pepper then set it aside.
3. Whisk the remaining ingredients in a small bowl to make the marinade then toss them in a large bowl with the broccoli.
4. Airfry the broccoli for 10 to 14 min then serve it warm and enjoy.

Beetroot Chips

Serves: 2
Prep Time: 25 min
Ingredients:

- 3 medium beetroots, thinly sliced
- 2 teaspoons of vegetable oil
- Salt

Directions:

1. Preheat the Airfryer on 356 F for 5 min.
2. Toss the beet root slices with vegetable oil and a pinch of salt in a large bowl then airfry it for 12 to 18 min.
3. Once the time is up, serve your chips and enjoy.

Luncheon Fries

Serves: 2
Prep Time: 20 min
Ingredients:
- 1 can of luncheon meat, cut into thick stripes

Directions:

1. Preheat the Airfryer on 365 F for 5 min.
2. Airfry the luncheon sticks for 10 to 15 min then serve them warm and enjoy.

Glazed Cauliflower Bites

Serves: 2
Prep Time: 30 min
Ingredients:

- The florets of 1 small cauliflower
- 1/3 cup of plain flour
- 1/3 cup of gluten free oats
- 1/3 cup of shredded fresh coconut
- 1 egg, beaten
- 2 tablespoons of honey
- 2 tablespoons of soy sauce
- 1 teaspoon of garlic, puréed
- 1 teaspoon of Italian seasoning
- ½ teaspoon of mustard powder
- Black pepper
- Salt

Directions:

1. Preheat the Airfryer on 356 F for 5 min.
2. Mix the coconut with flour, mustard, oats and a pinch of salt in a small bowl and set it aside.
3. Season the cauliflower florets with the Italian seasoning, a pinch of salt and pepper.
4. Toss the cauliflower florets in a large bowl with the beaten egg then mix it with the oats mix.
5. Airfry the cauliflower for 15 min then stir it and cook it for another 5 min.
6. Mix honey with soy sauce and garlic in a small bowl then toss it with the cauliflower bites while they are warm.
7. Serve your glazed cauliflower bites warm and enjoy.

Crunchy Bacon Shrimp

Serves: 16 pieces
Prep Time: 10 min
Ingredients:

- 1 ¼ pound of medium shrimp, 16 shrimp peeled and deveined
- 1 pound of bacon, 16 thin slices
- Black pepper
- Salt

Directions:

1. Preheat the Airfryer on 390 F for 3 min.
2. Wrap a slice of bacon around each shrimp then refrigerate them for 20 min.
3. Once the time is up, airfry then wrapped bacon shrimp for 5 to 7 min then serve it warm and enjoy.

Cod Fish Bites

Serves: 2 to 4
Prep Time: 20 min
Ingredients:

- 1 pound of cod fish, cut into medium size dices
- 1 cup of purpose flour
- ¾ cup of breadcrumbs
- 2 eggs, lightly beaten
- 2 tablespoons of olive oil
- Black pepper
- Salt

Directions:

1. Preheat the Airfryer on 390 F for 3 min.
2. Mix the breadcrumbs with olive oil, a pinch of salt and pepper in a small bowl.
3. Dust the cod fish dices in flour then dip them in the beaten egg and roll them in the breadcrumbs.
4. Airfry the codfish dices for 8 to 10 min then serve them and enjoy.

Buttermilk Biscuits

Serves: 10
Prep Time: 20 min
Ingredients:

- 1 ¼ cup of purpose flour
- ½ cup of cake flour
- ¾ cup of buttermilk
- 4 tablespoons of butter, diced
- 1 teaspoon of granulated sugar
- ½ teaspoon of baking powder
- ¼ teaspoon of baking soda
- Salt

Directions:

1. Preheat the Airfryer on 400 F for 5 min.
2. Combine the baking soda with purpose flour, sugar, baking powder and cake flour in a large bowl then add in the butter with a pinch of salt and knead them until they are incorporated.
3. Add in the remaining ingredients and mix them until you get a soft dough then roll it on a floured surface until you get a 1 ½ inch thick disk.
4. Cut the dough with a cookie cutter into 10 disks.
5. Place the dough disks in a greased baking pan and brush them with some melted butter then airfry them for 8 min.
6. Once the time is up, serve your biscuits and enjoy.

Shirred Eggs

Serves: 2 to 3
Prep Time: 25 min
Ingredients:

- 4 large eggs
- 3 tablespoons of parmesan cheese, grated
- 2 thin slices of ham
- 2 tablespoons of heavy cream
- 2 teaspoons of butter, unsalted
- 1/8 teaspoon of paprika
- Black pepper
- Salt

Directions:

1. Preheat the Airfryer on 320 F for 5 min.
2. Whisk the 1 egg with the heavy cream, paprika, a pinch of salt and pepper in a mixing bowl.
3. Butter a small baking pan and lay in it the 2 ham slices then pour the egg cream mix all over it.
4. Crack the remaining eggs on them and season them with a pinch of salt and pepper then sprinkle on them the parmesan cheese.
5. Airfry the shirred eggs for 12 min then serve it warm and enjoy.

Crusty Fish Fingers

Serves: 2
Prep Time: 25 min
Ingredients:

- 2 thick white fish fillet
- 2 ounces of plain flour
- ½ cup of whole meal breadcrumbs
- 1 egg, beaten
- 3 tablespoons of fresh lemon juice
- 1 tablespoon of parsley, finely chopped
- 1 tablespoon of mixed herbs
- 1 tablespoon of fresh thyme, finely chopped
- Black pepper
- Salt

Directions:

1. Preheat the Airfryer on 356 F for 5 min.
2. Mix the bread crumbs with parsley and a pinch of salt.
3. Combine the fish with lemon juice, herbs, thyme, a pinch of salt and pepper in a food processor then blend them smooth.
4. Shape the fish mix into a fish finger sand roll them in the plain flour then dip them in the beaten egg and roll them in the breadcrumbs.
5. Airfry the fish finger for 8 min then serve them warm and enjoy.

British Crunchy Sausages

Serves: 4
Prep Time: 20 min
Ingredients:

- 4 thick sausages
- 1 cup of plain flour
- 1 cup of whole meal bread crumbs
- 1 egg, beaten
- 1 tablespoon of olive oil
- Black pepper
- Salt

Directions:

1. Preheat the Airfryer on 356 F for 5 min.
2. Season the breadcrumbs with a pinch of salt and pepper.
3. Dust the sausages in the flour then dip them in the beaten egg and roll them in the breadcrumbs.
4. Airfry the sausages for 15 min then serve them warm and enjoy.

Cheddar Bites

Serves: 6
Prep Time: 15 min
Ingredients:
- 1 pound of bacon, thinly sliced
- 1 pound of sharp cheddar cheese, cut into 6 equal pieces
- 1 cup of breadcrumbs
- 1 cup of purpose flour
- 4 tablespoons of olive oil
- 2 eggs, lightly beaten
- Black pepper
- Salt

Directions:

1. Preheat the Airfryer on 390 F for 3 min.
2. Mix the breadcrumbs with oil in a small bowl.
3. Wrap to slices of bacon around each piece of cheddar then refrigerate them for 5 min.
4. Dust the cheddar bites with flour then dip them in the beaten eggs and roll them in the breadcrumbs.
5. Airfry the cheddar bites for 5 to 7 min then serve them warm and enjoy.

Mini Portobello Pizza

Serves: 4
Prep Time: 10 min
Ingredients:

- 4 Portobello mushroom caps
- 16 small slices of pepperoni
- 4 tablespoons of tomato sauce
- 4 tablespoons of mozzarella, shredded
- 2 tablespoons of olive oil
- ¼ teaspoon of dry Italian seasoning
- Black pepper
- Salt

Directions:

1. Preheat the Airfryer on 330 F for 3 min.
2. Brush both sides of the mushroom caps with olive oil then season them with the Italian seasoning, a pinch of salt and pepper.
3. Spread the tomato sauce on the back of the mushroom caps then top them with pepperoni and mozzarella.
4. Airfry the mushroom caps for 4 to 5 min then serve them warm and enjoy.

Eggplant Patties

Serves: 12 to 14
Prep Time: 25 min
Ingredients:

- 15 ounces of ricotta cheese
- 3 medium eggplant, thinly sliced
- 10 basil leaves
- 1 cup of mozzarella cheese
- ½ cup of parmesan cheese, grated
- 1 egg
- 3 eggs, beaten
- 1 cup of purpose flour
- Breadcrumbs
- Black pepper
- Salt

Directions:

1. Preheat the Airfryer on 356 F for 3 min.
2. Season the eggplants slices from both sides with some salt then allow them to sit for 30 min.
3. Combine the parmesan cheese with ricotta, and mozzarella, basil, 1 egg, a pinch of salt and pepper in a mixing bowl and mix them.
4. Spread 1 tablespoon of the cheese mix on an eggplant slice then cover it with another slice and place it on a lined up baking sheet.
5. Repeat the process with the remaining ingredients then freeze them for 1 h.
6. Dust the frozen eggplant patties in some purpose flour then dip them in the beaten eggs and coat them with the breadcrumbs.
7. Airfry the eggplant patties for 12 to 16 min or until they become golden brown then serve them and enjoy.

Veggies Skewers

Serves: 12
Prep Time: 25 min
Ingredients:

- 3 potato, cooked and mashed
- 1 cup of mixed fresh veggies, finely chopped
- ½ cup of mozzarella, shredded
- ¼ cup of fresh mint, roughly chopped
- 1 inch of fresh ginger, peeled
- 2 tablespoons of corn flour
- 3 cloves of garlic
- ½ teaspoon of garam masala
- Black pepper
- Salt

Directions:

1. Preheat the Airfryer on 400 F for 5 min.
2. Cook the potatoes and mash them then set them aside.
3. Combine the remaining ingredients in a food processor and blend them smooth.
4. Transfer the veggies mix to a large mixing bowl with the mashed potato, a pinch of salt and pepper then knead them to incorporate the flavors.
5. Shape the veggies mix into 12 balls then press each ball to a wooden skewer.
6. Brush them with some vegetable oil then airfry them for 10 min.
7. Once the time is up, serve your veggies skewers and enjoy.

Rice Gratin

Serves: 4
Prep Time: 45 min
Ingredients:

- 3 cups of rice, cooked
- 1 large veal sausage, sliced
- 1 cup of milk
- ¼ cup of white cheese, shredded
- 3 tablespoons of broccoli florets
- 3 tablespoons of cheddar cheese, shredded
- 2 tablespoons of mozzarella cheese, shredded
- 2 tablespoons of carrot, diced
- 2 tablespoons of corn flour
- 1 tablespoon of butter
- 4 cloves of garlic, minced
- Black pepper
- Salt

Directions:

1. Preheat the Airfryer on 356 for 5 min.
2. Bring the milk in a saucepan to a boil and stir into it the white cheese until it completely melts then add in the corn flour and whisk them until no lumps are found to make the sauce.
3. Melt the butter in a large pan and sauté in it the garlic for 2 min then add in the broccoli with carrot and cook them for 5 min.
4. Stir in the sausage and cook them for 3 min then stir in the rice.
5. Pour the rice mix in a greased baking dish that fits in your Airfryer.
6. Pour the sauce all over the rice mix and sprinkle the shredded cheddar with mozzarella on top.
7. Airfry the gratin for 10 to 12 min then serve it warm and enjoy.

Chicken Skewers

Serves: 4
Prep Time: 35 min
Ingredients:

- 18 ounces of chicken breasts, diced
- 3 bell peppers, cut into chunks
- 1 cup of cherry tomatoes
- 1 cup of plain yogurt
- 2 tablespoons of cumin
- 2 teaspoons of olive oil
- 1 teaspoon of turmeric
- Black pepper
- Salt

Directions:

1. Preheat the Airfryer on 400 for 5 min.
2. Mix all the ingredients in a large bowl then season them with a pinch of salt and pepper.
3. Refrigerate the chicken for 2 h to an overnight to absorb the marinade.
4. Thread the cherry tomato with chicken dices and bell peppers dices into wooden skewers while alternating between them.
5. Airfry the skewers in the Airfryer for 14 to 16 min while turning them halfway through cooking.
6. Serve your chicken skewers warm and enjoy.

Airfried Eggs and Ham Breakfast

Serves: 4
Prep Time: 35 min
Ingredients:

- 18 ounces of baby spinach
- 4 ounces of ham, sliced
- 4 eggs
- 1 tablespoon of olive oil
- 4 teaspoons of full cream milk
- Black pepper
- Salt

Directions:

1. Preheat the Airfryer on 356 for 5 min.
2. Heat the olive oil in a large pan and sauté in it the baby spinach for 4 min.
3. Place the cooked spinach in 4 greased remaking then top them with the ham, 1 egg and1 teaspoon of milk.
4. Season them with a pinch of salt and pepper then airfry them for 15 to 20 min.
5. Once the time is up, serve your breakfast ramekins warm and enjoy.

Sticky Pork Strips

Serves: 6
Prep Time: 25 min
Ingredients:
- 6 pork loin chops, cut into strips
- 2 tablespoons of soy sauce
- 2 tablespoons of honey
- 1 teaspoon of balsamic vinegar
- 1 clove of garlic, minced
- ¼ teaspoon of ginger
- Black pepper
- Salt

Directions:

1. Season the pork strips with a pinch of salt and pepper then set them aside.
2. Whisk the remaining ingredients in a small bowl to make the marinade then toss in the pork strips and allow them to marinate for 2 h to an overnight.
3. Drain the pork strips and airfry them for 6 to 8 min then serve them warm and enjoy.

English Breakfast

Serves: 4
Prep Time: 25 min
Ingredients:

- 7 ounces of baby spinach
- 8 chestnut mushrooms
- 8 tomatoes
- 8 bacon slices
- 4 eggs
- Black pepper
- Salt

Directions:

1. Preheat the Airfryer on 400 F for 5 min.
2. Season the mushroom and tomato with a pinch of salt then airfry them for 10 min.
3. In the meantime, heat 1 tablespoon of olive oil in large pan and cook in it the spinach of 3 to 4 min.
4. Cook the bacon in the same pan until they are crisp and set them aside then cook the eggs the way you like them.
5. Serve your English breakfast warm and enjoy.

Fish Frittata

Serves: 2
Prep Time: 30 min
Ingredients:

- 6 eggs
- 2 smoked trout fillets, flaked
- 1 small yellow onion, finely chopped
- 3 tablespoons of fresh dill, roughly chopped
- 2 tablespoons of olive oil
- Black pepper
- Salt

Directions:

1. Preheat the Airfryer on 320 F for 5 min.
2. Heat the oil in a large frying pan and sauté in it the onion for 2 min.
3. Whisk the eggs in a bowl with a pinch of salt and pepper then add to it the cooked onion with the remaining ingredients.
4. Pour the mix in a small baking dish and airfry it for 20 min.
5. Once the time is up, serve your frittata warm and enjoy.

Cheesy Muffins

Serves: 4
Prep Time: 25 min
Ingredients:

- 3.5 ounces of purpose flour
- 1.5 ounces of parmesan cheese, grated
- 1 egg
- 5 tablespoons of milk
- 2 tablespoons of vegetable oil
- 1 teaspoon of baking powder
- 1/8 teaspoon of Worcestershire sauce
- 1 pinch of mustard powder
- Black pepper
- Salt

Directions:

1. Preheat the Airfryer on 400 F for 5 min.
2. Beat the egg in a mixing bowl then add in the milk and oil and whisk them again.
3. Stir in the remaining ingredients one at a time until no lumps are found then pour the batter into a greased 4 cases muffin baking dish.
4. Airfry the muffins in the Airfryer for 15 min until they become golden brown then serve them and enjoy.

Spring Prawns Rolls

Serves: 4
Prep Time: 15 min
Ingredients:

- 12 spring roll wrappers
- 3.5 ounces of prawns, cooked
- 2 ounces of mushroom
- 1 ounce of bean sprouts
- 1 ounce of chestnuts, sliced
- 1 carrot, cut into matchsticks
- 1 spring onion, peeled and sliced
- 1 tablespoon of olive oil
- 1 tablespoon of soy sauce
- 1 tablespoon of fresh ginger, grated
- 1 teaspoon of Chinese five spice powder
- Black pepper
- Salt

Directions:

1. Preheat the Airfryer on 400 F for 5 min.
2. Heat the oil in a large pan and sauté in it the mushroom with ginger and water chestnuts for 2 min.
3. Add in the remaining ingredients except for the wrappers and cook them for 1 min then turn off the heat and allow them to cool down completely.
4. Divide the prawns mix on the spring roll wrappers and wrap them then airfry them for 5 to 8 min or until they become golden brown.
5. Serve your spring prawns rolls warm and enjoy.

Cheesy Baked Potato

Serves: 4
Prep Time: 35 min
Ingredients:

- 4 large potatoes
- 1/3 cup of cottage cheese
- 1 tablespoon of whole grain mustard
- Black pepper
- Salt

Directions:

1. Preheat the Airfryer on 400 F for 5 min.
2. Wash the potatoes and airfry them for 25 min until they become soft.
3. Halve the potato and scoop them flesh gently without ruining the skin into a large mixing bowl.
4. Add into it the remaining ingredients with a pinch of salt and pepper then scoop it back into the potato skin.
5. Serve your potato warm and enjoy.

Spinach and Ricotta Parcels

Serves: 4
Prep Time: 12 min
Ingredients:

- 6 sheets of filo pastry
- 21 ounces of baby spinach
- 12 ounces of ricotta cheese
- 1 egg beaten
- The zest of 1 lemon
- 1 teaspoon of olive oil
- Black pepper
- Salt

Directions:

1. Preheat the Airfryer on 400 F for 5 min.
2. Heat the oil in a large pan and cook in it the spinach of 3 to 4 min then allow it cool down completely.
3. Mix the spinach with remaining ingredients in a large bowl to make the filling.
4. Cut each filo pastry into 3 strips then fill each strip with 1 tablespoon of the filling then fold them gently.
5. Brush each filo parcel with some oil then airfry them for 4 to 6 min or until they become golden brown.
6. Serve your spinach and ricotta parcels warm and enjoy.

Roasted Raisins and Brussels Sprouts Salad

Serves: 4
Prep Time: 35 min
Ingredients:

- 14 ounces of Brussels sprouts
- 2 ounces of raisins
- 2 ounces of pine nuts, toasted
- The zest and juice of 1 orange
- 1 tablespoon of olive oil
- Black pepper
- Salt

Directions:

1. Preheat the Airfryer on 400 F for 5 min.
2. Bring a pot of water to a boil and cook in it the Brussels sprouts for 4 min then drain them and place them in an ice bath.
3. Drain the Brussels sprouts and set them aside to cool down.
4. Pour the orange juice into a small bowl then soak in it the raisins for 20 min.
5. Toss the Brussels sprouts in a large bowl with the olive oil, a pinch of salt and pepper then airfry them for 15 min.
6. Once the time is up, toss the roasted Brussels sprouts with the raisins and orange juice and the remaining ingredients then serve them and enjoy.

Crunchy Potato Bacon Salad

Serves: 4 to 6
Prep Time: 35 min
Ingredients:

- 4 potatoes, peeled and cut into wedges
- 4 bacon fillets, roughly chopped
- 1 tablespoon of olive oil
- 2 sprigs of rosemary
- 4 cloves of garlic
- Black pepper
- Salt

Directions:

1. Preheat the Airfryer on 400 F for 5 min.
2. Toss all the ingredients in a large bowl then airfry them for 25 to 30 min.
3. Serve your crunchy potato salad warm and enjoy.

Potato Samosa

Serves: 4 to 6
Prep Time: 35 min
Ingredients:

- 2 large potato, cooked and mashed
- 2 cups of purpose flour
- 1 cup of fresh green peas
- 2 tablespoons of vegetable oil
- 2 teaspoons of garam masala
- 1 teaspoon of ghee, melted
- 1 teaspoon of water
- 1 teaspoon of mixed garlic and ginger paste
- 1 teaspoon of turmeric
- 1 teaspoon of red chili powder
- 1 teaspoon of Salt

Directions:

1. Preheat the Airfryer on 365 F for 3 min.
2. Combine the water with ghee, flour and a pinch of salt in a large bowl then mix them and knead until you get a soft dough.
3. Cover the dough with a cling film and allow it to rest for 30 min.
4. Combine the remaining ingredients in a large bowl and mix them the filling.
5. Roll the dough on a floured surface then cut into circles.
6. Place 1 tablespoon of the filling on half of the small circle of dough then cover it with the other half and seal the edges with a fork.
7. Repeat the process with the remaining ingredients and brush them with some vegetable oil then airfry the potato samosa for 18 to 20 min.
8. Serve your potato samosa warm and enjoy.

Roasted Shishito Peppers with Goat Cheese

Serves: 20
Prep Time: 10 min
Ingredients:
- 6 ounces f shishito peppers
- 1 cup of goat cheese, crumbled
- 1 teaspoon of vegetable oil

Directions:

1. Preheat the Airfryer on 390 F for 5 min.
2. Toss the shishito peppers in a mixing bowl with vegetable oil then airfry for 5 min.
3. Crumble the goat cheese all the peppers then serve them and enjoy.

Cheddar and Cheese Stromboli

Serves: 4
Prep Time: 25 min
Ingredients:

- 1 pound of chicken breasts, thinly sliced
- 14 ounces of pizza dough
- 1 ¼ cup of cheddar cheese, grated
- ½ cup of any cheese sauce
- 1 tablespoon of Worcestershire sauce
- 1 teaspoon of vegetable oil
- Black pepper
- Salt

Directions:

1. Preheat the Airfryer on 400 F for 3 min.
2. Toss the onion with oil in a large bowl then airfry it for 8 min.
3. Once the time is up, add the Worcestershire sauce with chicken, a pinch of salt and pepper then cook them for another 8 min.
4. Transfer the chicken onion mix into a plate then allow them to cool down completely.
5. Roll the dough on a floured surface then sprinkle half of the cheddar cheese all over it leaving 1 inch empty from all sides.
6. Top it with the chicken and onion mix followed by the cheese sauce and the remaining cheddar cheese.
7. Lower the Airfryer temperature to 370 F.
8. Roll the dough gently while tucking the filling inside then shape into a U and cut 4 slits on it with a sharp knife.
9. Brush the Stromboli with some vegetable oil then airfry it for 12 min.
10. Serve your Stromboli warm and enjoy.

Roasted Veggies and Pasta Salad

Serves: 6 to 8
Prep Time: 25 min
Ingredients:

- 1 pound of penne pasta, cooked 1 pound of penne pasta, cooked
- 4 ounces of mushroom, halved
- 1 cup of cherry tomato, halved
- 1 orange bell pepper, cut into chunks
- 1 red bell pepper, cut into chunks
- 1 green bell pepper, cut into chunks
- 1 zucchini, halved and sliced
- 1 yellow squash, halved and sliced
- ¼ cup of olive oil
- 3 tablespoons of balsamic vinegar
- 1 teaspoon of Italian seasoning
- Black pepper
- Salt

Directions:

1. Preheat the Airfryer on 380 F for 5 min.
2. Toss the mushroom with bell peppers, squash and zucchini, 2 tablespoons of olive oil, and Italian seasoning, a pinch of salt and pepper in a large bowl then airfry them for 10 to 12 min.
3. Transfer the roasted veggies to a large bowl with the remaining ingredients then refrigerate until it cools down then serve it and enjoy.

Roasted Fig Salad

Serves: 2 to 3
Prep Time: 16 min
Ingredients:

- 8 fresh figs, halved
- 3 cups of arugula
- 1 ½ cups of chickpeas, cooked
- 3 tablespoons of balsamic vinegar
- 2 tablespoons of olive oil
- 1 teaspoon of vegetable oil
- Salt

Directions:

1. Preheat the Airfryer on 365 F for 5 min.
2. Toss the figs halves in a large bowl with 1 tablespoon of balsamic vinegar then airfry it for 5 to 7 min.
3. Pour the juices that came out from the figs in a small bowl then add in the olive oil with a pinch of salt and whisk it to make the dressing.
4. Heat the vegetable oil in a large pan and sauté in it the chickpeas for 1 min.
5. Lay then arugula in a large serving plate then top it with the chickpeas followed by the roasted figs.
6. Drizzle the dressing all over the salad then serve it and enjoy.

Green Beans and Almonds Salad

Serves: 4
Prep Time: 30 min
Ingredients:
- 1 ½ pounds of fresh green beans
- ½ pound of shallots, peeled and quartered
- ¼ cup of almonds, silvered
- 2 tablespoons of olive oil
- Black pepper
- Salt

Directions:

1. Preheat the Airfryer on 400 F for 5 min.
2. Bring a salted pot of water to a boil and cook in it the beans for 2 min then drain it and set it aside.
3. Toss the green beans with olive oil, shallots, a pinch of salt and pepper in a large bowl then Airfry them for 25 min.
4. Once the time is up, add in the slivered almonds then serve your salad warm and enjoy.

Crunchy Radish Salad

Serves: 4
Prep Time: 40 min
Ingredients:

- 1 ½ pounds of fresh radish
- ½ pound of mozzarella, sliced
- 2 tablespoons of balsamic vinegar
- 2 tablespoons of olive oil
- Black pepper
- Salt

Directions:

1. Preheat the Airfryer on 350 F for 5 min.
2. Wash the radish and pat it dry then toss it in a large bowl with olive oil, a pinch of salt and pepper.
3. Place the radish in the Airfryer and cook them for 30 min.
4. Once the time is up, toss the radish with mozzarella and balsamic vinegar then serve it right away and enjoy.

Ham and Mushroom Quiche

Serves: 2 to 4
Prep Time: 45 min
Ingredients:
- 9 inches store bought pie dough
- 1 ounces of button mushroom, finely chopped
- 1/3 cup of heavy cream
- 1/3 cup of gruyere cheese, grated
- ¼ cup of yellow onion, diced
- 3 eggs
- 2 tablespoons of ham, diced
- 1 tablespoon of butter, unsalted
- ¼ teaspoon of fresh thyme, finely chopped
- 1/8 teaspoon of nutmeg powder
- Black pepper
- Salt

Directions:

1. Preheat the Airfryer on 400 F for 5 min.
2. Place the pie dough in a greased and floured baking pan and trim its edges until you get an 8 inches pie shell.
3. Cover the pie dough with a parchment paper and fill it with some dry beans then airfry it for 10 min.
4. Once the time is up, discard the parchment paper and set the pie shell aside to cool down completely.
5. Melt the butter in a large pan and sauté in it the mushroom for 4 min then add in the ham with onion and cook them for 4 min.
6. Turn off the heat and pour the mix into the pie shell.
7. Whisk the eggs in a mixing bowl with the heavy cream, nutmeg powder, thyme, a pinch of salt and pepper then pour them all over the mushroom mix in the pie shell.
8. Sprinkle the cheese all over the pie.
9. Preheat the Airfryer on 300 F for 5 min.
10. Airfry the quiche of 30 min then serve it warm and enjoy.

83

Roasted Mediterranean Veggies

Serves: 4
Prep Time: 25 min
Ingredients:

- 1 large green pepper, cut into chunks
- 1 large courgette, cut into chunks
- 1 large parsnip, sliced
- 1 large carrot, sliced
- 1 cup of cherry tomato, halved
- 6 tablespoons of olive oil
- 1 tablespoon of honey
- 2 teaspoons of garlic, puréed
- 1 teaspoon of mustard
- ½ teaspoon of dry herbs
- Black pepper
- Salt

Directions:

1. Preheat the Airfryer on 356 F for 5 min.
2. Toss all the ingredients in a large bowl and airfry them for 15 min.
3. Once the time is up, stir them and raise the temperature to 400 F then cook them for 4 min.
4. Serve your roasted veggies warm and enjoy.

Mushroom Stir Fry

Serves: 4
Prep Time: 15 min
Ingredients:

- 9 ounces of mushroom, quartered
- 1 green capsicum, finely chopped
- ½ red capsicum, seeded and cut into chunks
- 1 tablespoon of water
- ½ tablespoon of garlic ginger paste
- Salt

Directions:

1. Preheat the Airfryer on 400 F for 3 min.
2. Toss all the ingredients in a large bowl then airfry them for 10 min.
3. Once the time is up, serve your mushroom stir fry warm and enjoy.

Potato Gratin

Serves: 6
Prep Time: 45 min
Ingredients:
- 7 russet potato, peeled and sliced
- ½ cup of gruyere cheese, grated
- ½ cup of heavy cream
- ½ cup of milk
- ½ teaspoon of nutmeg powder
- Black pepper
- Salt

Directions:

1. Preheat the Airfryer on 390 F for 3 min.
2. Whisk the cream with milk, nutmeg, a pinch of salt and pepper in a large mixing bowl then stir in the sliced potatoes.
3. Pour the potato mix in a greased baking dish and airfry it for 25 min then sprinkle the cheese all over it and cook it for 10 min.
4. Once the time is up, serve your gratin warm and enjoy.

Crispy Spring Rolls

Serves: 8
Prep Time: 16 min
Ingredients:
- 4 ounces of chicken breasts, cooked and shredded
- 8 spring roll wrappers
- 1 carrot, sliced
- 1 stalk of celery, sliced
- ½ cup of mushroom, sliced
- 1 egg, lightly beaten
- 1 teaspoon of cornstarch
- 1 teaspoon of sugar
- ½ teaspoon of vegetable oil
- ½ teaspoon of fresh ginger, grated
- Black pepper
- Salt

Directions:

1. Preheat the Airfryer on 390 F for 3 min.
2. Mix the egg with cornstarch in a small bowl then set it aside.
3. Mix the mushroom with chicken, celery, carrot, sugar and ginger in a large mixing bowl with a pinch of salt and pepper.
4. Place 1/8 of the filling in a spring roll wrapper then wrap it and seal it with the egg mix.
5. Repeat the process with the remaining ingredients.
6. Airfry the wrappers for 3 to 4 min until they become golden then serve them and enjoy.

Roasted Feta Tomato Layers

Serves: 4
Prep Time: 25 min
Ingredients:

- 2 large heirloom tomatoes, thickly sliced
- 8 ounces of feta cheese, thickly sliced
- ½ cup of red onion, thinly sliced
- 1 tablespoon of olive oil
- Black pepper
- Salt

Directions:

1. Preheat the Airfryer on 390 F for 3 min.
2. Heat the oil in a large pan then sauté in it the onion with a pinch of salt for 3 to 4 min then set it aside to cool down completely.
3. Place a slice of tomato and top it with another slice of feta cheese then top them with some of the cooked onion.
4. Repeat the process with the remaining ingredients then season them with a pinch of salt and pepper.
5. Place feta tomato layers in the Airfryer and airfry them for 12 to 14 min then serve them warm and enjoy.

Steak and Egg Rolls

Serves: 4
Prep Time: 25 min
Ingredients:

- 2 packages of frozen steak, sliced
- 1 package of egg roll wrappers
- ½ pound of provolone cheese, diced
- 1 white onion, finely chopped
- 1green bell pepper, finely chopped
- 1 tablespoon of olive oil
- Black pepper
- Salt

Directions:

1. Preheat the Airfryer on 350 F for 3 min.
2. Heat the oil in a large pan then sauté in it the bell pepper with onion for 3 to 4 min.
3. Heat a splash of olive oil in another pan and cook in it the steak slices until they are done.
4. Mix the cheese with cooked steak and onion mix then allow them to cool down completely to make the filling.
5. Place ¼ cup of the filling in the middle of a wrapper then fold it and repeat the process with the remaining ingredients.
6. Airfry the wrappers for 10 min then raise the temperature to 390 and cook them for another 4 min.
7. Once the time is up, serve your rolls warm with some hot sauce and enjoy.

Tropical Hawaiian Tortilla

Serves: 2
Prep Time: 20 min
Ingredients:
- 4 ounces of ham, diced
- 2 tortillas
- 1 cup of fresh pineapple, diced
- ½ cup of mozzarella cheese, shredded
- 1/3 cup of tomato sauce

Directions:

1. Preheat the Airfryer on 356 F for 3 min.
2. Spread the tomato sauce on both tortillas then top them with the ham followed by the pineapple and mozzarella cheese.
3. Airfry each tortilla for 4 to 6 min then serve them warm and enjoy.

Cheesy Bacon Cake

Serves: 4 to 6
Prep Time: 1 h
Ingredients:

- 10 ounces of bacon, diced
- 7 cups of baguette bread, diced
- 2 cups of cheddar cheese, grated
- 1 ¼ cup of milk
- 6 eggs
- Black pepper
- Salt

Directions:

1. Preheat the Airfryer on 356 F for 3 min.
2. Cook the bacon in a large bowl until it becomes crispy then drain it and set it aside.
3. Whisk the milk with eggs, a pinch of salt and pepper in a large mixing bowl.
4. Place the bread in a large zip lock bag and pour the egg and milk mix all over it followed by 1 ½ cup of cheese and the cooked bacon.
5. Mix the gently then seal the bag and allow them to rest for 2 h to an overnight so that the bread can absorb the egg mix.
6. Pour the mix in a greased bacon pan and bake it for 30 to 35 min then serve it and enjoy.

Double Coated McCain Veggies Fingers

Serves: 2 to 3
Prep Time: 25 min
Ingredients:

- 1 package of McCain veggies fingers
- 3 eggs, beaten
- 1 cups of breadcrumbs
- ½ cup of parmesan cheese, grated
- 1 teaspoon of Italian seasoning
- Black pepper
- Salt

Directions:

1. Preheat the Airfryer on 356 F for 3 min.
2. Mix the breadcrumbs with parmesan, Italian seasoning, a pinch of salt and pepper in a mixing bowl.
3. Dip the frozen veggies finger in the beaten eggs then roll them in the breadcrumbs mix.
4. Airfry the veggies fingers for 14 to 16 min then serve them and enjoy.

Tomatillo Sausage Ratatouille

Serves: 4
Prep Time: 45 min
Ingredients:

- 30 ounces of canned butterbeans, drained
- 30 ounces of canned tomato, chopped
- 8 pork sausages
- 4 courgettes
- 2 eggplants
- 2 bell peppers
- 2 red onions
- 2 tablespoons of balsamic vinegar
- 2 tablespoons of olive oil
- 2 cloves of garlic, minced
- 4 sprigs of thyme
- Black pepper
- Salt

Directions:

1. Preheat the Airfryer on 400 F for 5 min.
2. Toss the eggplant with bell peppers, courgettes and red onion in a large bowl then roast them in the Airfryer for 20 min.
3. Remove the veggies from the Airfryer and allow them to cool down.
4. Preheat the Airfryer on 356 F.
5. Airfry the sausages for 12 to 15 min.
6. Once the time is up, dice the roasted veggies with sausages then transfer them into a large saucepan and bring them to a simmer.
7. Adjust the seasoning of the ratatouille then serve it warm and enjoy.

Creamy Corn Pudding

Serves: 6 to 8
Prep Time: 1 h 25 min
Ingredients:

- 4 ounces of Monterey Jack cheese, grated
- 3 cups of bread, diced
- 2 cups of corn kernels
- 1 ½ cup of whole milk
- 3 eggs
- 4 strips of bacon, diced
- ¾ cup of yellow onion, diced
- ½ cup of heavy cream
- ½ cup of red bell pepper, diced
- ¼ cup of celery, diced
- 3 tablespoons of parmesan cheese, grated
- 1 tablespoon of butter
- 2 teaspoons of garlic, minced
- 1 teaspoon of fresh thyme leaves
- ¼ teaspoon of cayenne pepper
- Black pepper
- Salt

Directions:

1. Preheat the Airfryer on 320 F for 5 min.
2. Cook the bacon in a small pan that fits in your Airfryer until it becomes golden brown then drain it and set it aside.
3. Add in the corn kernels and cook it for 10 min then stir in the onion with bell pepper, celery and cook them for 5 min.
4. Add the thyme with garlic and turn off the heat then transfer the mix to a large mixing bowl.

5. Add the eggs with milk and heavy cream then whisk them.
6. Fold in the Monterey cheese with bread, cayenne pepper and a pinch of salt then pour the mix into a greased small pan that fits in your Airfryer.
7. Airfry the pudding for 30 min.
8. Once the time is up, sprinkle the parmesan cheese all over the pudding then airfry it for another 30 min then serve your pudding warm and enjoy.

Mac and Cheese Wheel

Serves: 4 to 6
Prep Time: 45 min
Ingredients:

- ½ pound of elbow pasta
- ½ cup of gruyere cheese
- ½ cup of cheddar cheese, grated
- ½ cup of heavy cream
- ½ cup of fontina cheese
- ½ cup of milk
- ¼ cup of parmesan cheese, grated
- ¼ cup of bread crumbs
- 1 tablespoon of butter, melted
- 1/8 teaspoon of nutmeg powder
- Black pepper
- Salt

Directions:

1. Preheat the Airfryer on 350 F for 5 min.
2. Cook the pasta according to the directions on the package.
3. Drain the pasta and place it in a large bowl then add in the cheese except for the parmesan with nutmeg powder, cream, a pinch of salt and pepper.
4. Mix the parmesan cheese with butter and bread crumbs.
5. Pour the pasta into a small pan that fits in your Airfryer then sprinkle the crumbs all over it and airfry it for 30 min.
6. Once the time is up, allow the mac and cheese wheel to cool down for 20 min then serve it and enjoy.

Airfried Meatballs

Serves: 3 to 4
Prep Time: 15 min
Ingredients:

- 12 ounces of lean beef, minced
- 1 small yellow onion, finely chopped
- 1 egg
- 3 tablespoons of breadcrumbs
- 1 tablespoon of fresh parsley, finely chopped
- ½ tablespoon of fresh thyme leaves
- Black pepper
- Salt

Directions:

1. Preheat the Airfryer on 390 F for 3 min.
2. Mix all the ingredients in a large bowl with a pinch of salt and pepper then knead them with your hands for 1 min.
3. Shape the mix into 10 to 12 meatballs then airfry them for 8 to 10 min.
4. Once the time is up, serve your meatballs warm and enjoy.

Moroccan Meatballs

Serves: 4
Prep Time: 20 min
Ingredients:

- 1 pound of lean lamb, minced
- 4 ounces of lean turkey, minced
- ¼ cup of olive oil
- 1 egg white
- 1 ½ tablespoon of parsley, finely chopped
- 1 teaspoon of cayenne pepper
- 1 teaspoon of cumin
- 1 teaspoon of red chili paste
- Black pepper
- Salt

Directions:

1. Preheat the Airfryer on 390 F for 3 min.
2. Combine all the ingredients in a large bowl with a pinch of salt and pepper then knead them with your hands to incorporate the flavors.
3. Shape the mix into medium size meatballs then airfry them for 6 to 8 min.
4. Once the time is up, serve your meatballs warm with some tomato or yogurt sauce and enjoy.

Tropical Korean Satay

Serves: 2
Prep Time: 15 min
Ingredients:

- 12 ounces of chicken tenders
- ½ cup of fresh pineapple juice
- ½ cup of light soy sauce
- ¼ cup of sesame oil
- 1 tablespoon of fresh ginger, minced
- 4 cloves of garlic, minced
- Black pepper
- Salt

Directions:

1. Preheat the Airfryer on 390 F for 3 min.
2. Season the chicken tenders with a pinch of salt and pepper then toss them in a large bowl and refrigerate them for 2 h.
3. Drain the chicken tenders and pat them dry then airfry them for 6 to 8 min.
4. Once the time is up, serve your chicken tenders warm and enjoy.

Cheesy Meatballs Biscuits

Serves: 2
Prep Time: 35 min
Ingredients:

- 1 can of biscuits dough
- 10 meatballs, cooked and halved (check the recipes above)
- 20 small mozzarella dices
- 1 tablespoon of parmesan cheese, grated
- ½ teaspoon of Italian seasoning
- ¼ teaspoon of garlic powder
- Black pepper
- Salt

Directions:

1. Preheat the Airfryer on 356 F for 3 min.
2. Cut each biscuit into 2 layers.
3. Press 1 mozzarella dice into ½ meatball then place it in a biscuit half and wrap it around it.
4. Repeat the process with the remaining ingredients.
5. Place the stuffed biscuits in a greased baking pan that fits in your Airfryer.
6. Mix the Italian seasoning with garlic powder, parmesan cheese, a pinch of salt and pepper in a small bowl.
7. Sprinkle the cheese mix all over the biscuits then airfry them for 20 to 25 min.
8. Once the time is up, serve your biscuits and enjoy.

Red Lentils Stew with Chickpea Galettes

Serves: 4
Prep Time: 1 h 25 min
Ingredients:

- 28 ounces of canned tomato, chopped
- 6 ounces of chickpea flour
- 6 ounces of red lentils
- 1 large yellow onion, finely chopped
- 2 small white onions, finely chopped
- ¼ cup of fresh lemon juice
- 2 inches of fresh ginger, peeled and minced
- 2 tablespoons of vegetable oil
- 2 teaspoons of garam masala
- 3 teaspoons of turmeric
- 2 teaspoons of cumin
- 1 teaspoon of yellow mustard seeds
- 2 cloves of garlic, minced
- Black pepper
- Salt

Directions:

1. Heat the oil in a large deep pan and sauté in it the garlic with yellow onion for 10 min on low heat.
2. Add 2 teaspoons of garam masala with mustard seeds, ginger, lentils and tomato then simmer them for 40 min on low heat.
3. Mix the chickpea flour with lemon juice, a pinch of salt, 1 teaspoon of turmeric, cumin and white onion in a large bowl until they form a dough while adding water.
4. Shape the dough into small balls then flatten them and airfry them for 10 min to make the Galettes.
5. Serve your chicken stew with the chickpea galettes and enjoy.

Salmon Cakes

Serves: 4
Prep Time: 10 min
Ingredients:

- 14 ounces of mashed potato
- 9 ounces of salmon, cooked
- 1.5 ounces of plain flour
- 1 handful of parsley, finely chopped
- 1 tablespoon of capers, drained
- The zest of 1 lemon
- Black pepper
- Salt

Directions:

1. Preheat the Airfryer on 365 F for 5 min.
2. Combine all the ingredients except for the flour in a large mixing bowl and mix them with your hands then shape them into 4 fishcakes.
3. Dust the fish cakes with the flour then airfry them for 7 min until they become golden.
4. Once the time is up, serve your salmon cakes with some plain yogurt and enjoy.

Crusty Chicken Escallops

Serves: 4
Prep Time: 12 min
Ingredients:

- 4 chicken breasts
- 2.5 ounces of panko breadcrumbs
- 1.5 ounces of plain flour
- 1.5 ounces of parmesan cheese, grated
- 2 eggs, beaten
- 6 sage leaves, finely chopped
- Black pepper
- Salt

Directions:

1. Preheat the Airfryer on 400 F for 5 min.
2. Cover the chicken breasts with a piece of Clingfilm then pound them with a rolling pin until they become ¼ inch thick.
3. Mix the cheese with breadcrumbs and sage then set them aside.
4. Season the chicken breasts with a pinch of salt and pepper then dust them with the flour, dip them in the beaten eggs and coat them with the breadcrumbs.
5. Spray the chicken breasts with some oil then airfry them for 4 to 6 min or until they become golden.
6. Serve your chicken escallops warm and enjoy.

Crusty Chicken Tenders

Serves: 4
Prep Time: 25 min
Ingredients:

- ¾ pound of chicken tenders
- 2 eggs, beaten
- ½ cup of purpose flour
- ½ cup of breadcrumbs
- 2 tablespoons of olive oil
- Black pepper
- Salt

Directions:

1. Preheat the Airfryer on 330 F for 3 min.
2. Mix the breadcrumbs with olive oil, a pinch of salt and pepper.
3. Dust the chicken tenders with flour then dip them in the beaten eggs and roll them in the breadcrumbs.
4. Airfry the chicken tenders for 10 min then raise the temperature to 390 F and cook them for another 5 min.
5. Once the time is up, serve your chicken tenders with some hot sauce and enjoy.

Salmon Patties

Serves: 8
Prep Time: 15 min
Ingredients:

- 1 pound of fresh salmon, diced
- 1 cup of breadcrumbs
- ½ cup of celery, finely chopped
- 1/3 cup of fresh cilantro, finely chopped
- ¼ cup of onion, finely chopped
- 1 egg white
- 2 tablespoons of vegetable oil
- 1 tablespoon of fresh lemon juice
- Black pepper
- Salt

Directions:

1. Preheat the Airfryer on 400 F for 3 min.
2. Combine all the ingredients in a food processor with a pinch of salt and pepper then pulse them few times until they become minced.
3. Shape the mix into 8 patties then refrigerate them for 30 min.
4. Once the time is up, airfry the salmon cake on batches for 4 to 8 min per batch then serve them warm and enjoy.

Sesame Chicken Wings

Serves: 4 to 8
Prep Time: 30 min
Ingredients:
- 8 chicken drumsticks
- 4 tablespoons of honey
- 2 tablespoons of olive oil
- 2 cloves of garlic, minced
- ½ tablespoon of fresh ginger, minced
- 3 teaspoons of light soy sauce
- 2 teaspoons of sesame seeds, toasted
- Black pepper
- Salt

Directions:

1. Preheat the Airfryer on 400 F for 5 min.
2. Season the chicken drumsticks with a pinch of salt and pepper then place them in a large zip lock bag with the remaining ingredients except for the sesame seeds.
3. Place the chicken drumsticks in the fridge for 2 h to an overnight.
4. Once the time is up, drain the chicken drumsticks and airfry them for 10 min.
5. Lower the temperature to 356 F and cook them for another 10 min.
6. Sprinkle the sesame seeds all over the chicken drumsticks then serve them and enjoy.

Singapore Chicken Wings

Serves: 8
Prep Time: 25 min
Ingredients:

- 8 chicken wings
- 2 tablespoons of corn flour
- ½ tablespoon of cooking wine
- 1 teaspoon of fresh ginger, grated
- 1 teaspoon of sesame oil
- ½ teaspoon of sugar
- Black pepper
- Salt

Directions:

1. Preheat the Airfryer on 356 F for 2 min.
2. Toss all the ingredients in a large bowl and allow them to marinade for 30 min.
3. Airfry the chicken wings for 8 min then flip them and fry them for another 8 min.
4. Serve your chicken wings with a hot sauce and enjoy.

Jerk Chicken Wings

Serves: 6
Prep Time: 25 min
Ingredients:
- 3 pounds of chicken wings
- ½ cup of red wine vinegar
- 5 tablespoons of fresh lime juice
- 2 tablespoons of brown sugar
- 2 tablespoons of soy sauce
- 2 tablespoons of olive oil
- 1 tablespoon of ground allspice
- 6 cloves of garlic, finely chopped
- 1 tablespoon of fresh ginger, minced
- 1 teaspoon of cayenne pepper
- 1 teaspoon of cinnamon
- Black pepper
- Salt

Directions:

1. Preheat the Airfryer on 390 F for 3 min.
2. Season the chicken wings with a pinch of salt and pepper.
3. Toss all the ingredients in a large bowl then transfer them into a large zip lock bag and refrigerate it for 2 h.
4. Drain the chicken wings and airfry them for 16 to 18 min then serve them warm and enjoy.

Crusty Sesame Fish Fillets

Serves: 6
Prep Time: 16 min
Ingredients:

- 6 fresh white fish fillets
- 1 cup of purpose flour
- 1 cup of breadcrumbs
- 1 handful of sesame seeds, toasted
- 2 eggs, beaten
- ¼ teaspoon of dry rosemary
- Black pepper
- Salt

Directions:

1. Preheat the Airfryer on 400 F for 3 min.
2. Mix the breadcrumbs with rosemary, sesame seeds, a pinch of salt and pepper in a mixing bowl.
3. Season the fish fillets with a pinch of salt and pepper.
4. Dust the fish fillets with flour then dip them in the beaten eggs and coat them with the sesame breadcrumbs mix.
5. Airfry the fish fillets for 8 min then flip them and cook them for another 2 min.
6. Serve your fish fillets warm and enjoy.

White Fish Fillets with Lemon Sauce

Serves: 4
Prep Time: 40 min
Ingredients:

- 4 white fish fillets
- 1 cup of purpose flour
- ¼ cup of sugar
- ¼ cup of fresh lemon juice
- 1 egg white
- 4 teaspoons of corn flour
- 2 teaspoons of vegetable oil
- 3 teaspoon of chili sauce
- Black pepper
- Salt

Directions:

1. Preheat the Airfryer on 360 for 5 min.
2. Bring ½ cup of water in a saucepan to a boil then stir into it the sugar until it dissolves.
3. Mix the flour with chili sauce, egg white and vegetable oil in a small bowl then add 3 tablespoons of water and whisk them until they make a thick paste.
4. Season the fish fillets with a pinch of salt and pepper then dip them in the flour batter.
5. Place the fish fillet in a greased Airfryer and airfry them for 15 to 20 min.
6. In the meantime, add the corn flour with a pinch of salt and the lemon juice to the water and sugar mix then cook them on low heat while stirring until they thicken to make the sauce.
7. Serve your fish fillets with the lemon sauce and enjoy.

Salmon Fillets with Courgettes Ribbons

Serves: 4
Prep Time: 20 min
Ingredients:

- 4 salmon fillets
- 4 large courgettes, spiralized
- 1 avocado, peeled
- 1 clove of garlic, peeled
- 2 tablespoons of fresh lemon juice
- Black pepper
- Salt

Directions:

1. Preheat the Airfryer on 356 for 5 min.
2. Combine the lemon juice with avocado and garlic in a food processor and blend them smooth to make the dressing.
3. Toss the courgette noodles with the avocado dressing then set it aside.
4. Airfry the salmon fillets for 10 min.
5. Once the time is up, serve your salmon fillets with the courgette noodles and enjoy.

Airfried Cod Fillets

Serves: 4
Prep Time: 15 min
Ingredients:

- 4 cod fish fillets
- 2 tablespoons of olive oil
- 2 tablespoons of fresh lemon juice
- Black pepper
- Salt

Directions:

1. Preheat the Airfryer on 356 F for 5 min.
2. Season the fish fillets with a pinch of salt and pepper then place them in the Airfryer.
3. Whisk the olive oil with lemon juice in a small bowl then drizzle them all over the fish fillets and airfry them for 8 to 10 min.
4. Serve your cod fillets warm and enjoy.

Asian Sea Bass

Serves: 2 to 3
Prep Time: 25 min
Ingredients:
- 1 medium sea bass, cut into chunks
- 1 large tomato, quartered
- 1 lime, sliced
- 3 slices of fresh ginger, diced
- 1 tablespoon of vegetable oil
- 2 cloves of garlic, peeled and minced
- Black pepper
- Salt

Directions:

1. Preheat the Airfryer on 356 F for 5 min.
2. Heat the oil in a pan then sauté in it the garlic with ginger for 1 min.
3. Arrange the fish chunks in a large piece of foil in the Airfryer then top it with the tomato and lime slices then drizzle the ginger and garlic oil mix on it.
4. Cover the fish with another piece of foil then cook it for 15 to 17 min.
5. Once the time is up, serve your fish warm and enjoy.

Dill Salmon

Serves: 4
Prep Time: 30 min
Ingredients:
- 4 pieces of salmon, 6 ounces each
- 2 tablespoons of fresh dill, finely chopped
- 1 tablespoon of olive oil
- Black pepper
- Salt

Directions:

1. Preheat the Airfryer on 270 F for 3 min.
2. Season the salmon pieces with a pinch of salt and pepper.
3. Mix the olive oil with dills in a small bowl then brush the salmon pieces with them.
4. Airfry them salmon pieces for 20 to 25 min then serve them warm and enjoy.

Teriyaki Halibut Steak

Serves: 2
Prep Time: 20 min
Ingredients:

- 1 pound of halibut steak
- 2/3 cup of light soy sauce
- ½ cup of cooking wine
- ¼ cup of fresh orange juice
- ¼ cup of sugar
- 2 tablespoons of fresh lime juice
- 1 clove of garlic, crushed
- Black pepper
- Salt

Directions:

1. Season the halibut steak with a pinch of salt and pepper.
2. Combine the remaining ingredients in a small saucepan and bring them to a boil then simmer it until it reduces by half to make the marinade.
3. Place the halibut steak in a zip lock bag and pour the marinade all over it then seal it and refrigerate it for 30 min.
4. Once the time is up, drain the steak and airfry it for 10 to 12 min then serve it warm and enjoy.

Coconut Chicken Legs

Serves: 4
Prep Time: 45 min
Ingredients:
- 4 whole chicken legs
- ½ cup of coconut milk
- 2 ounce of fresh ginger, peeled and minced
- 5 teaspoons of turmeric powder
- Black pepper
- Salt

Directions:

1. Preheat the Airfryer on 380 for 5 min.
2. Season the chicken legs with a pinch of salt and pepper.
3. Combine the turmeric with ginger and coconut milk in a food processor and blend them smooth to make the marinade.
4. Rub the chicken legs with the marinade then allow them to sit for 4 h to an overnight.
5. Airfry each chicken leg in the Airfryer one at a time for 20 to 25 min then serve them warm and enjoy.

Crunchy Buttermilk Chicken Breasts

Serves: 4
Prep Time: 45 min
Ingredients:

- 4 chicken breasts halves
- 17 ounces of panko breadcrumbs
- 2 cups of buttermilk
- ½ cup of plain flour
- 2 eggs, beaten
- 2 teaspoons of garlic, minced
- 1 teaspoon of cayenne pepper
- Black pepper
- Salt

Directions:

1. Preheat the Airfryer on 365 for 5 min.
2. Mix the cayenne pepper with garlic and buttermilk in a large bowl then dip in it the chicken breasts and allow them to marinate for an overnight.
3. Drain the chicken breasts from the marinade and dust them in the flour mix then dip them in the eggs and roll them in the breadcrumbs.
4. Airfry the chicken for 20 to 25 min then serve it and enjoy.

Paprika Chicken Legs

Serves: 4
Prep Time: 45 min
Ingredients:

- 4 chicken legs
- 2 teaspoons of smoked paprika
- 1 teaspoon of honey
- ½ teaspoon of garlic powder
- Black pepper
- Salt

Directions:

1. Preheat the Airfryer on 400 for 5 min.
2. Mix the honey with paprika and garlic powder in a small bowl.
3. Season the chicken legs with a pinch of salt and pepper then score them with a knife before rubbing them with the paprika mix.
4. Airfry the chicken legs for 35 to 40 min then serve them warm and enjoy.

Honey Chicken

Serves: 2 to 3
Prep Time: 40 min
Ingredients:

- 18 ounces of chicken pieces
- 1 ½ tablespoon of honey
- 1 ½ tablespoon of whole grain mustard
- 1 tablespoon of light soy sauce
- 2 tablespoons of fresh lemon juice
- ¼ teaspoon of dry rosemary
- Black pepper
- Salt

Directions:

1. Preheat the Airfryer on 320 F for 5 min.
2. Season the chicken with a pinch of salt and pepper.
3. Whisk the remaining ingredients in a small bowl to make the marinade.
4. Place the chicken in a zip lock bag and pour the marinade all over it then seal it and allow it to marinade for 30 min.
5. Airfry the chicken for 18 min then increase the temperature to 356 F and cook the chicken for another 18 min.
6. Once the time is up, serve your chicken warm and enjoy.

Teriyaki Chicken

Serves: 4
Prep Time: 45 min
Ingredients:

- 4 chicken thighs, boneless
- 6 tablespoons of teriyaki sauce
- 2 tablespoons of cooking wine
- 2 teaspoons of fresh ginger, grated
- Black pepper
- Salt

Directions:

1. Preheat the Airfryer on 356 F for 5 min.
2. Season the chicken with a pinch of salt and pepper then transfer it to a zip lock bag with the remaining ingredients and allow it marinate for 30 min to 1 h.
3. Place the 2 chicken thighs with half of the remaining marinade in the Airfryer and airfry them for 8 min.
4. Once the time is up, increase the temperature to 380 F and fry them for another 7 min.
5. Repeat the process with the remaining 2 chicken thighs then serve them warm and enjoy.

Chicken Tandoori

Serves: 4
Prep Time: 35 min
Ingredients:

- 4 chicken legs
- 3 tablespoons of fresh lemon juice
- 3 teaspoons of garlic, puréed
- 3 teaspoon of fresh ginger, minced
- 2 teaspoons of red chili powder
- 1 teaspoon of cumin
- 1 teaspoon of turmeric
- 1 teaspoon of garam masala
- Black pepper
- Salt

Directions:

1. Preheat the Airfryer on 320 F for 3 min.
2. Make few slits in the chicken legs with a sharp knife then season them with a pinch of salt and pepper.
3. Mix the remaining ingredients in a small bowl then rub the chicken legs with it and let them sit for 1 to 2 h.
4. Airfry the chicken legs for 20 to 24 min then serve it warm and enjoy.

Stuffed Cheesy Burgers

Serves: 2
Prep Time: 30 min
Ingredients:

- 2 burger buns
- 12 ounces of lean beef, minced
- 4 slices of cheddar cheese, cut into chunks
- 3 tablespoons of yellow onion, minced
- 1 tablespoon of ketchup
- 2 teaspoons of yellow mustard
- Black pepper
- Salt

Directions:

1. Preheat the Airfryer on 370 F.
2. Mix the lean beef with mustard, ketchup, onion, a pinch of salt and pepper in a mixing bowl.
3. Shape the beef mix into 4 patties then wet your hands with some water and flatten them.
4. Place half of the cheese on 1 patties then cover it with the other one and pinch the edges to keep the cheese inside then repeat the process with the other 2 patties.
5. Airfry the burger patties for 20 min then serve them with your favorite toppings and enjoy.

Burger King

Serves: 4
Prep Time: 35 min
Ingredients:

- 14 ounces of lean pork, minced
- 4 burger buns
- ½ small avocado, mashed
- 1 small yellow onion, diced
- 1 tablespoon of tomato ketchup
- 1 tablespoon of Worcestershire sauce
- 1 teaspoon of parsley, finely chopped
- 1 teaspoon of dry thyme
- 1 teaspoon of garlic, puréed
- Black pepper
- Salt

Directions:

1. Preheat the Airfryer on 356 F for 10 min.
2. Mix the mashed avocado with garlic, thyme and parsley, Worcestershire sauce, tomato ketchup and pork in a large bowl then shape them into 4 burger patties.
3. Airfry the burgers for 10 to 12 min.
4. Assemble your avocados then serve them with your favorite toppings and enjoy.

Chicken King Burgers

Serves: 4
Prep Time: 25 min
Ingredients:

- 6 chicken breasts
- 1 cup of breadcrumbs
- 1 cup of plain flour
- 1 egg, beaten
- 1 teaspoon of paprika
- 1 teaspoon of Worcestershire sauce
- 1 teaspoon of mustard powder
- Black pepper
- Salt

Directions:

1. Preheat the Airfryer on 356 F for 5 min.
2. Combine the chicken breasts with mustard, paprika, a pinch of salt, pepper and Worcestershire sauce in a food processor and blend them smooth.
3. Shape the chicken mix into 4 patties then airfry them for 15 min.
4. Once the time is up, serve your chicken burgers with your favorite toppings and enjoy.

Classic Fried Cheese Burgers

Serves: 6
Prep Time: 20 min
Ingredients:
- 6 burger buns
- 1 pound of lean beef, minced
- 6 cheddar cheese slices
- ¼ cup of yellow onion, finely chopped
- 1 tablespoon of fresh parsley, finely chopped
- ½ teaspoon of paprika
- 1/8 teaspoon of cinnamon
- Black pepper
- Salt

Directions:

1. Preheat the Airfryer on 390 F for 3 min.
2. Combine the lean beef with onion, paprika, cinnamon, a pinch of salt and pepper in a mixing bowl then knead them with your hands to incorporate the flavors.
3. Shape the mix into 6 patties and airfry them for 10 to 12 min then assemble your burger with the cheese slices and enjoy.

Roasted Pork

Serves: 4 to 6
Prep Time: 1 h 20 min
Ingredients:

- 2 pounds of pork belly
- 2 teaspoons of garlic powder
- 1 ½ teaspoons of dry rosemary
- 1 ½ teaspoons of five spice powder
- 1 teaspoon of Black pepper
- 1 teaspoon of Salt

Directions:

1. Preheat the Airfryer on 320 for 5 min.
2. Bring a salted pot of water to a boil then cook in it the pork belly for 12 min then drain it and pat it dry and let it rest for 3 h.
3. Mix the remaining ingredients in a small bowl then rub the pork belly with it and airfry it for 30 min.
4. Once the time is up, turn the heat to 365 F then airfry the pork belly for another 25 min.
5. Serve your pork belly and enjoy.

Airfried Beef Roast

Serves: 4 to 6
Prep Time: 1 h
Ingredients:

- 2 Pounds of beef roast
- 2 teaspoons of olive oil
- Black pepper
- Salt

Directions:

1. Preheat the Airfryer on 356 for 5 min.
2. Rub the roast with olive oil then season it with a pinch of salt and pepper.
3. Place the roast in the Airfryer and Airfry it for 30 to 45 min or until it is done to your liking.
4. Serve you roast warm and enjoy.

Herbed Lamb Chops

Serves: 2 to 4
Prep Time: 40 min
Ingredients:

- 2 pound rack of lamb
- ¼ cup of panko bread crumbs
- 2 tablespoons of fresh herbs de province, finely chopped
- 2 tablespoons of parmesan cheese, grated
- 1 tablespoon of olive oil
- 1 tablespoon of Dijon mustard
- The zest of 1 lemon
- Black pepper
- Salt

Directions:

1. Preheat the Airfryer on 400 for 5 min.
2. Pierce the rack of lamb all over with a knife then season it with a pinch of salt and pepper.
3. Mix the remaining ingredients in a small bowl and coat the rack of lamb with it.
4. Airfry the rack of lamb for 20 to 30 min then serve it warm and enjoy.

Garam Masala Lamb Chops

Serves: 4
Prep Time: 20 min
Ingredients:

- 4 lamb chops
- 4 tablespoons of plain yogurt
- 2 tablespoons of fresh lemon juice
- 2 teaspoons of garam masala
- 1 teaspoon of cumin seeds
- Black pepper
- Salt

Directions:

1. Preheat the Airfryer on 400 F for 5 min.
2. Season the lamb chops with a pinch of salt and pepper then set them aside.
3. Whisk the remaining ingredients in a small bowl to make the marinade and rub the lamb chops with it.
4. Refrigerate the lamb chops for 2 h to an overnight to absorb the marinade then airfry them for 10 to 14 min.
5. Serve your lamb chops warm and enjoy.

Classic Beef Roast

Serves: 6 to 8
Prep Time: 1 h 10 min
Ingredients:

- 3 pounds beef roast
- 2 tablespoons of olive oil
- 2 teaspoon of dry Italian seasoning
- 2 clove of garlic, minced
- Black pepper
- Salt

Directions:

1. Preheat the Airfryer on 320 F for 5 min.
2. Season the beef roast with a pinch of salt and pepper.
3. Mix the garlic with olive oil and Italian seasoning in a small bowl then rub the roast with them.
4. Airfry the roast for 30 min then turn it and cook it for another 30 min.
5. Once the time is up, serve your beef roast with some roasted veggies and enjoy.

Marinated Skirt Steak

Serves: 2
Prep Time: 20 min
Ingredients:
- 1 pound skirt steak, cut into 2 portions
- 1 cup of fresh parsley, finely chopped
- ¾ cup of olive oil
- 3 tablespoons of red wine vinegar
- 2 tablespoons of fresh oregano, finely chopped
- 1 tablespoon of cumin
- 2 teaspoons of paprika
- 1 teaspoon of cayenne pepper
- 3 cloves of garlic, finely chopped
- Black pepper
- Salt

Directions:

1. Preheat the Airfryer on 390 F for 3 min.
2. Season the steak with a pinch of salt and pepper.
3. Mix the remaining ingredients in a small bowl to make the sauce.
4. Pour ¼ cup of the sauce in a zip lock bag with the 2 steak portion then seal it and refrigerate it for 2 h.
5. Once the time is up, airfry the 2 steak portions for 8 to 12 min then serve them warm with the remaining sauce and enjoy.

Strawberry Tarts

Serves: 9
Prep Time: 20 min
Ingredients:

- 8 ounces of plain flour
- 3.5 ounces of butter
- 1 ounce of caster sugar
- Strawberry Jam
- Water
- Salt

Directions:

1. Preheat the Airfryer on 356 F for 5 min.
2. Mix the flour with butter, a pinch of salt and caster sugar in a small bowl until they become crumbly then add in enough water until you get a firm dough.
3. Roll the dough on a floured surface then cut it into 9 small disks and press each disk into a greased pastry case.
4. Fill each pastry case with 2 to 3 teaspoons of strawberry jam then airfry them for 10 min.
5. Allow the tarts to cool down completely then serve them and enjoy.

Vanilla Shortbread

Serves: 4
Prep Time: 25 min
Ingredients:

- 9 ounces of plain flour
- 6 ounces of butter
- 2.5 ounces of caster sugar
- 1 drop of vanilla essence
- Salt

Directions:

1. Preheat the Airfryer on 356 F for 5 min.
2. Mix all the ingredients in a large bowl then knead them with your hands until they become creamy.
3. Roll the bread on a floured surface then cut them into a medium size disks with a cookie cutter.
4. Airfry the shortbread of 12 min then serve it with your favorite toppings and enjoy.

Chocolate Bites

Serves: 9
Prep Time: 25 min
Ingredients:

- 9 ounces of plain flour
- 6 ounces of butter
- 2.5 ounces of caster sugar
- 9 chocolate chunks
- 2 tablespoons of cocoa powder
- 1 teaspoon of vanilla extract
- Salt

Directions:

1. Preheat the Airfryer on 356 F for 5 min.
2. Mix the cocoa powder with flour and sugar in a small bowl.
3. Add in the butter and knead them until you get a smooth dough then shape it into 9 balls.
4. Press each chocolate chunk into the middle of each ball then airfry them for 8 min.
5. Lower the temperature to 320 then cook them for another 5 min.
6. Allow the chocolate bites to cool down completely then serve them and enjoy.

Stuffed Banana S'mores

Serves: 4
Prep Time: 10 min
Ingredients:
- 4 large bananas
- 3 tablespoons of mini peanut butter chips
- 3 tablespoons of graham cracker cereal
- 3 tablespoons of mini sweet chocolate chips
- 3 tablespoons of mini marshmallows

Directions:

1. Preheat the Airfryer on 400 F for 5 min.
2. Slice the bananas lengthwise gently without cutting the bottom peel then open them slightly.
3. Fill each banana with the chocolate chips followed by the peanut butter chips, marshmallows and cereal.
4. Airfry the bananas for 6 min and allow them to cool down a bit then serve them and enjoy.

Crunchy Peanut Fluff Triangles

Serves: 4
Prep Time: 15 min
Ingredients:

- 4 sheet of filo pastry sheets
- 2 ounces of butter
- 4 tablespoons of chunky peanut butter
- 4 teaspoons of marshmallow fluff

Directions:

1. Preheat the Airfryer on 390 F for 3 min.
2. Place a sheet of pastry on a working surface and brush it with some butter then top it with another sheet of pastry and brush it with butter and repeat the process with the 3 and fourth sheets.
3. Cut the stack of philo sheets into 4 triangles.
4. Place 1 tablespoon of peanut butter on a triangle of the filo sheet then top it with 1 teaspoon of marshmallow fluff and fold it.
5. Repeat the process with the remaining 3 triangles.
6. Brush the stuffed triangles with the remaining butter then airfry them for 3 to 5 min until they become golden and crunchy.
7. Serve your crunchy peanut fluff triangles and enjoy.

Lemon Biscuits

Serves: 9
Prep Time: 15 min
Ingredients:

- 8 ounces of caster sugar
- 8 ounces of butter
- 1 egg
- The juice of 1 small lemon
- The zest of 1 small lemon
- 1 teaspoon of vanilla extract
- Salt

Directions:

1. Preheat the Airfryer on 356 F for 5 min.
2. Mix the sugar with butter and flour in a large bowl until they become crumbled.
3. Add in the remaining ingredients knead them until you get a soft dough.
4. Roll the dough on a floured surface then cut into medium sized biscuits and airfry them for 5 min.
5. Once the time is up, serve your biscuits and enjoy.

Coffee Muffins

Serves: 12
Prep Time: 25 min
Ingredients:

- 2 cups of purpose flour
- 1 cup of strong brewed coffee, cold
- ½ cup of semi sweet chocolate chips
- 1/3 cup of sugar
- 1/3 cup of brown sugar
- 8 tablespoons of butter
- 1 egg
- 1 tablespoon of baking powder
- 1 tablespoon of instant espresso powder
- ½ teaspoon of vanilla extract
- ½ teaspoon of cinnamon
- Salt

Directions:

1. Preheat the Airfryer on 356 F for 10 min.
2. Whisk the brewed coffee with butter, vanilla and egg in a mixing bowl.
3. Mix the remaining ingredients in a large mixing bowl then stir into them the coffee mix until no lumps are found.
4. Fill 4/5 silicon muffin molds with the batter then airfry them for 8 to 10 min.
5. Allow the muffins to cool down completely then serve them and enjoy.

Lychee Muffins

Serves: 10 to 12
Prep Time: 16 min
Ingredients:

- 1 ½ cup of purpose flour
- 1 cup of fresh lychee, roughly chopped
- 1/3 cup of vegetable oil
- 1/3 cup of milk
- 1/3 cup of fresh banana, mashed
- ¼ cup of sugar
- 2 teaspoons of baking powder
- 2 teaspoons of vanilla extract
- Salt

Directions:

1. Preheat the Airfryer on 356 F for 10 min.
2. Mix the flour with sugar, a pinch of salt and baking powder in a mixing bowl.
3. Mix the vanilla with milk, banana and vegetable oil in a large mixing bowl then stir in the flour mix until no lumps are found.
4. Fold in the lychee then spoon the batter into greased muffin cases and airfry them for 8 to 10 min.
5. Allow the muffins to cool down completely then serve them and enjoy.

Lime Cupcakes

Serves: 6
Prep Time: 30 min
Ingredients:

- 9 ounces of plain Greek yogurt
- 7 ounces of cream cheese
- 2 eggs
- 1 egg yolk
- The juice of 2 limes
- The zest of limes, grated
- 1 teaspoon of vanilla extract
- Salt

Directions:

1. Preheat the Airfryer on 356 F for 5 min.
2. Mix the cream cheese with yogurt in a mixing bowl until they become creamy.
3. Add in the sugar and mix them then stir in the remaining ingredients with a pinch of salt.
4. Pour the batter into 6 greased cupcake cases and refrigerate the remaining batter.
5. Airfry the cupcakes for 10 min then raise the temperature to 365 F and cook them for another 10 min.
6. Allow the cupcakes to cool down completely then garnish them with the remaining batter.
7. Serve your cupcakes and enjoy.

Green Tea Cupcakes

Serves: 2
Prep Time: 35 min
Ingredients:

- 1 cup of purpose flour
- 2 eggs
- 6 tablespoons of plain yogurt
- 3 tablespoons of sugar
- 2 tablespoons of honey
- 2 tablespoons of canola oil
- 2 teaspoons of green matcha powder
- 2 teaspoons of baking powder
- Salt

Directions:

1. Preheat the Airfryer on 356 F for 10 min.
2. Mix the baking powder with flour and a pinch of salt.
3. Whisk the oil with egg in a mixing bowl until they become pale then add in the honey with yogurt and mix them again.
4. Add in the sugar while mixing all the time.
5. Fold in the flour mix until no lumps are found then add in the matcha powder and fold it in as well until no lumps are found.
6. Spoon the batter into greased muffin cases and airfry them for 8 to 12 min.
7. Allow the cupcakes to cool down completely then serve them and enjoy.

Chocolate Muffins

Serves: 6
Prep Time: 20 min
Ingredients:

- ½ cup of self raising flour
- ¼ cup of sugar
- 4 tablespoons of milk
- 2 tablespoons of yogurt
- 2 tablespoons of chocolate chips
- 2 tablespoons of coconut oil
- 1 tablespoon of honey
- 1 tablespoon of cocoa powder
- 1 teaspoon of apple cider vinegar
- ½ teaspoon of vanilla extract
- ¼ teaspoon of baking soda
- Salt

Directions:

1. Preheat the Airfryer on 400 F for 5 min.
2. Combine the flour with cocoa powder, baking soda, sugar and a pinch of salt and in a large bowl.
3. Whisk the milk with yogurt, honey, coconut oil and vanilla in a small bowl then stir it into the apple cider until no lumps are found.
4. Stir in the chocolate chips then pour the batter into 6 greased lined up silicone cupcakes liners.
5. Airfry the muffins for 8 min.
6. Once the time is up, allow the muffins to cool down completely then serve them and enjoy.

Blueberries Muffins

Serves: 10 to 12
Prep Time: 25 min
Ingredients:

- 1 ½ cup of purpose flour
- 1 cup of fresh blueberries
- 1 cup of yogurt
- ½ cup of white sugar
- 1/3 cup of vegetable oil
- 1 egg
- 2 teaspoons of vanilla extract
- 2 teaspoons of baking powder
- Salt

Directions:

1. Preheat the Airfryer on 356 F for 10 min.
2. Mix the baking powder with flour, sugar and a pinch of salt.
3. Whisk the oil with egg, vanilla extract and yogurt in a small mixing bowl.
4. Add the egg and yogurt mix into the flour mix and mix them until no lumps are found.
5. Fold in the blueberries then pour the batter into greased muffin cases.
6. Airfry the muffins for 10 to 12 min then serve them and enjoy.

Airfried Sweet Bread

Serves: 18
Prep Time: 1 h 20 min
Ingredients:
- 18 ounces of purpose flour
- 1 cup of milk
- 2 eggs
- 4 ounces of butter, softened
- 2 ¼ ounces of caster sugar
- 2 ¼ teaspoons of instant
- 1 ½ teaspoon of Salt

Directions:

1. Preheat the Airfryer on 320 for 5 min.
2. Combine all the ingredients in a large mixing bowl and mix them until you get a dough then transfer it to a floured surface and knead it with your hands for 5 to 7 min until the dough becomes soft.
3. Shape the dough into 18 balls.
4. Line the Airfryer basket with a piece of foil then brush its sides with some oil or a cooking spray.
5. Place half of the dough balls in the Airfryer basket and set the other balls in a lined up baking sheet.
6. Cover them with a damp cloth then allow them to rest until they double in their size for about 30 min.
7. Bake the first 9 buns in the Airfryer for 14 to 16 min.
8. Lower the temperature to 310 F and bake the second batch for 14 to 16 min as well.
9. Once the time is up, brush then sweet bread buns with some melted butter then serve them and enjoy.

Fried Velvet Cupcakes

Serves: 4
Prep Time: 35 min
Ingredients:

- 2 cups of purpose flour
- ¾ cup of peanut butter
- ¾ cup of icing sugar
- 3 eggs
- 2 teaspoons of red food coloring
- 1 teaspoon of cocoa powder
- 1 teaspoon of vanilla extract

Directions:

1. Preheat the Airfryer on 356 for 5 min.
2. Combine all the ingredients in a large bowl then mix them with an electric beater until no lumps are found.
3. Pour the batter into a silicon cupcakes mold then airfry them for 10 to 14 min.
4. Allow the cupcakes to cool down for 10 to 12 min.
5. Garnish your cupcakes with some cream cheese then serve them and enjoy.

Molten Chocolate Lava

Serves: 2 to 4
Prep Time: 25 min
Ingredients:

- 4.5 ounces of dark chocolate, finely chopped
- 4.5 ounces of butter
- 2.6 ounces of flour
- 2 ½ ounces of brown sugar
- The juice of ½ an orange
- 2/3 teaspoon of baking powder
- ½ teaspoon of instant coffee
- Salt

Directions:

1. Preheat the Airfryer on 356 for 5 min.
2. Combine the butter with chocolate in a double boiler and melt them completely then stir into them the orange juice.
3. Combine the coffee with eggs and sugar in a large mixing bowl and beat them until they become creamy then stir in the chocolate mix.
4. Stir in the baking powder with flour and a pinch of salt until no lumps are found.
5. Pour the batter into a small greased baking dish and airfry it for 10 min.
6. Serve your orange chocolate cake and enjoy.

Creamy Berries with French Toast

Serves: 2
Prep Time: 12 min
Ingredients:

- 2 thick slices of sourdough
- 1 cup of mixed fresh berries
- 1 cup of plain Greek yogurt
- 2 eggs
- 2 tablespoons of butter
- 1 tablespoon of honey
- 1 teaspoon of vanilla extract

Directions:

1. Preheat the Airfryer on 356 F for 5 min.
2. Spread the butter all over the 2 slices of sourdough bread and set them aside.
3. Whisk the vanilla and eggs in a small bowl then dip in it the bread slices and airfry them for 6 min.
4. Top the bread slices with yogurt and berries then serve them and enjoy.

Airfried Apples

Serves: 4
Prep Time: 15 min
Ingredients:

- 4 green apples, cored
- 1.5 ounces of mixed nuts
- 1.5 ounces of breadcrumbs
- 1 ounce of butter
- 2 tablespoons of brown sugar
- The zest of 1 orange
- 1 teaspoon of cinnamon powder

Directions:

1. Preheat the Airfryer on 356 F for 5 min.
2. Score the apples several times then set them aside.
3. Mix the remaining ingredients in a small bowl then fill the cored apples with them.
4. Airfry the apples for 10 min then serve them warm and enjoy.

Caramelized Honey Figs

Serves: 8
Prep Time: 15 min
Ingredients:

- 8 figs
- 1.5 ounces of butter
- 3 tablespoons of honey
- 1 teaspoon of rose water
- Salt

Directions:

1. Preheat the Airfryer on 356 F for 5 min.
2. Cut a cross on the figs and squeeze them slightly then top them with butter.
3. Place the figs in the Airfryer and drizzle the honey all over them then cook them for 5 min.
4. Serve your caramelized figs with some mascarpone cheese and enjoy.

Vanilla Semolina Cookies

Serves: 10 to 12
Prep Time: 45 min
Ingredients:

- 1 cup of purpose flour
- 1 cup of powdered sugar
- ½ cup of gram or corn flour
- ½ cup of semolina
- 1 tablespoon of ghee
- 1 teaspoon of vanilla extract
- Salt

Directions:

1. Preheat the Airfryer on 365 F for 3 min.
2. Mix the purpose flour with gram flour and semolina in a large mixing bowl then add to them the remaining ingredients and knead them with your hand until you get a soft dough while adding a little bit of water if needed.
3. Set the dough aside and cover it with a plastic wrap for 30 min.
4. Once the time is up, shape the dough into small cookies then garnish them with some pistachios or almonds.
5. Airfry the cookies on batches for 10 to 12 then serve them and enjoy.

Airfried Oreo Cake

Serves: 4
Prep Time: 20 min
Ingredients:

- 12 regular Oreo biscuits
- 1 cup of milk
- 1 tablespoon of almonds, silvered
- 1 teaspoon of baking powder
- ½ teaspoon of baking soda

Directions:

1. Preheat the Airfryer on 400 F for 3 min.
2. Place the Oreo cookies in a food process and process them until they become fine then transfer them into a large bowl with the remaining ingredients.
3. Mix all the ingredients with a spatula until no lumps are found then transfer it to a greased and lined up baking pan.
4. Airfry the cake for 8 min then serve it with some ice cream and enjoy.

Airfried Chocolate Soufflé

Serves: 2
Prep Time: 25 min
Ingredients:

- 3 ounces of semi sweet chocolate, finely chopped
- 2 egg yolks
- 2 egg whites
- ¼ cup of butter
- 3 tablespoons of sugar
- 2 tablespoons of purpose flour
- ½ teaspoon of vanilla extract
- Salt

Directions:

1. Preheat the Airfryer on 330 F for 5 min
2. Combine the butter with chocolate in a double boiler then melt them completely.
3. Beat the eggs in a mixing bowl until they become pale then add in the vanilla with sugar and beat them again.
4. Add in the melted chocolate butter with flour and whisk them until no lumps are found.
5. Beat the egg whites until their soft peaks then fold them gently into the batter.
6. Pour the batter into 2 greased ramekins then airfry them for 14 min.
7. Once the time is up, serve your soufflé with some ice cream and enjoy.

Apricot Berry Crumble

Serves: 6
Prep Time: 30 min
Ingredients:
- 18 fresh apricots, diced
- 1 cup of flour
- 5 ½ ounces of fresh mixed berries
- ½ cup of caster sugar
- 3 tablespoons of butter
- 1 tablespoon of cold water
- 2 tablespoons of fresh lemon juice
- Salt

Directions:

1. Preheat the Airfryer on 390 F for 3 min.
2. Toss the berries with lemon juice, 2 tablespoons of sugar and apricot in a large bowl.
3. Mix the flour with butter, cold water and a pinch of salt in a mixing bowl until they become crumbly.
4. Pour the fruits mix in a greased baking dish then top it with the crumbly flour mix.
5. Airfry the crumble for 20 min then serve it with some ice cream and enjoy.

Lemon and Vanilla Soufflé

Serves: 6
Prep Time: 1 h
Ingredients:

- 1 ounce of sugar
- 1 cup of milk
- ¼ cup of butter, softened
- ¼ cup of purpose flour
- ¼ cup of caster sugar
- 5 egg whites
- 4 egg yolks
- The zest of lemon, grated
- 2 teaspoons of vanilla extract
- 1 teaspoon of cream of tartar
- Salt

Directions:

1. Preheat the Airfryer on 390 F for 3 min.
2. Mix the flour with butter in a mixing bowl until they become like a paste.
3. Heat the milk in a saucepan and stir in the caster sugar until it dissolves then add in the lemon zest.
4. Bring the milk mix to a boil then add in the flour and butter paste.
5. Beat them until no lumps are found then simmer it until the mix thickens for few minutes.
6. Turn of the heat and allow the batter to cool down for 10 min.
7. Grease 6 (3 ounces) ramekin with some butter then set them aside.

8. Beat the eggs yolks with vanilla extract then add them to the milk batter and stir them vigorously until they no lumps are found.
9. Beat 1 ounce of sugar with the cream of tartar and egg whites until there soft peaks then fold them into the milk batter.
10. Pour the batter in the greased ramekins and airfry them for 14 to 16 min.
11. Serve your soufflé with your favorite toppings and enjoy.

Raspberry Soufflé

Serves: 6
Prep Time: 25 min
Ingredients:

- 17.5 ounces of fresh raspberries
- 3.5 ounces of sugar
- 6 egg whites
- 1 cup of castor sugar
- 2 tablespoons of icing sugar

Directions:

1. Preheat the Airfryer on 400 F for 3 min.
2. Place the raspberries in a food processor and purée them the pour it through a sieve.
3. Pour the raspberry juice in a saucepan and bring it to a boil then stir in the sugar until it completely dissolves.
4. Lower the heat and simmer the juice for 10 min.
5. Beat the egg whites with a pinch of salt and 3.5 ounces of sugar gradually until it soft peaks.
6. Fold 3 to 4 tablespoons of the cooked raspberry juice to the egg whites.
7. Grease 6 soufflé molds with some butter and dust them with icing sugar.
8. Pour the egg whites mix in the molds and bake them for 8 min then lower the heat to 356 F and bake them for 4 to 6 min.
9. Once the time is up, serve your soufflé and enjoy.

Fried Cinnamon Rolls

Serves: 8
Prep Time: 35 min
Ingredients:

- 1 pound of frozen bread dough, thawed
- 4 ounces of cream cheese, softened
- 1 ¼ cup of powdered sugar
- ¾ cup of brown sugar
- ¼ cup of butter
- 2 tablespoons of butter, melted
- 1 ½ tablespoon of cinnamon
- ½ teaspoon of vanilla extract

Directions:

1. Preheat the Airfryer on 350 F for 5 min
2. Roll the dough on a floured surface until it becomes 11 inches by 13 inches rectangular.
3. Brush the dough leaving 1 inches on all sides empty.
4. Mix the cinnamon with brown sugar in a small bowl then sprinkle it all over the dough leaving that 1 inch empty.
5. Roll the dough gently then cut into 8 long round pieces then set them aside to rise for 1 h 30 min.
6. Place rolls in the Airfryer and fry them for 5 min then turn them and fry them for another 4 min.
7. Repeat the process with the remaining 4 rolls.
8. Combine the butter with cream cheese in a small bowl then microwave them for 30 seconds.
9. Once the time is up, stir in the sugar into the cream cheese mix followed by the vanilla until no lumps are found to make the glaze.
10. Drizzle the glaze all over the cinnamon rolls while they are hot then serve them and enjoy.

Airfried Marble Cake

Serves: 4 to 6
Prep Time: 35 min
Ingredients:

- 4 ounces of self raising flour
- 3 ounces of caster sugar
- ¼ ounces of cocoa powder
- 3 eggs
- 1/3 cup of butter, melted
- ½ teaspoon of fresh lemon juice

Directions:

1. Preheat the Airfryer on 356 for 5 min.
2. Mix ¼ cup of melted butter and cocoa powder in a small bowl them set it aside.
3. Mix the remaining butter with caster sugar in a small bowl until they become pale then add in the flour with the eggs and lemon juice until no lumps are found.
4. Pour half of the cake batter into a greased baking pan that will fit in your airfyer and top it with cocoa and butter mix then cover it with the remaining batter and Airfry it for 15 to 8 min.
5. Allow the cake to cool down completely then serve it and enjoy.

Apricot and Cocoa Cake

Serves: 2 to 3
Prep Time: 30 min
Ingredients:
- 2 ounces of plain flour
- 2 ounces of caster sugar
- 2 ounces of butter
- 1 tablespoon of cocoa powder
- 1 tablespoon of apricot jam
- 1 egg
- Salt

Directions:

1. Preheat the Airfryer on 320 F for 5 min.
2. Beat the sugar with butter until they become creamy then add in the remaining ingredients and mix them until no lumps are found.
3. Pour the batter into a greased small baking dish then airfry it for 150 F.
4. Once the time is up, allow the cake to cool down completely then serve it and enjoy.

Frosted Carrot Cake

Serves: 4 to 6
Prep Time: 35 min
Ingredients:

- 9 ounces of icing sugar
- 9 ounces of self raising flour
- 5 ounces of brown sugar
- 2 ounces of butter
- ¾ cup of olive oil
- 2 large carrots, grated
- The juice of 1 small orange
- The zest of 1 small orange, grated
- 2 eggs
- 2 tablespoons of milk
- 1 teaspoon of mixed spice
- Salt

Directions:

1. Preheat the Airfryer on 356 F for 5 min.
2. Mix the carrot with flour, mixed spice and sugar in a large bowl then stir in the olive oil with milk and eggs.
3. Pour the batter into a greased baking tin and airfry it for 5 min then lower the temperature to 320 F and cook it for 5 min.
4. Melt the butter and pour in it a mixing bowl then stir in the orange juice with zest.
5. Add in the icing sugar and beat them until they become creamy to make the icing.
6. Allow the cake to cool down completely then cover it with the icing.
7. Serve your cake and enjoy.

Classic Chocolate Cake

Serves: 4 to 6
Prep Time: 1 h
Ingredients:

- 1 cup of purpose flour
- 2/3 cup of caster sugar
- ½ cup of sour cream
- 3 eggs
- 9 tablespoons of butter, unsalted
- 6 tablespoons of cocoa powder
- 2 teaspoons of vanilla extract
- 1 teaspoon of baking powder
- ½ teaspoon of baking soda
- Salt

Directions:

1. Preheat the Airfryer on 320 F for 3 min.
2. Combine all the ingredients in a food processor and blend them smooth then pour the batter in a greased baking dish.
3. Airfry the cake for 35 to 40 min.
4. Once the time is up, allow the cake to cool down completely then serve it with your favorite toppings and enjoy.

Apple Pie

Serves: 4 to 6
Prep Time: 45 min
Ingredients:

- 2 store bought pie crusts, defrosted
- 1 large apple, finely chopped
- 1 egg, beaten
- 2 tablespoons of sugar
- 1 tablespoon of raw sugar
- 1 tablespoon of butter
- 1 tablespoon of cinnamon
- 2 teaspoons of fresh lemon juice
- ½ teaspoon of vanilla extract

Directions:

1. Preheat the Airfryer on 320 F for 3 min.
2. Roll the pie crusts on a floured surface then adjust one of them in a greased baking pan that fits in your Airfryer.
3. Mix the remaining ingredients in a mixing bowl and pour them in the baking pan then cover them with the second pie crust.
4. Pierce several holes in the pie crust with a fork then airfry it for 30 min.
5. Once the time is up, serve your apple pie with some vanilla ice cream and enjoy.

Airfried Pecan Pie

Serves: 2 to 4
Prep Time: 45 min
Ingredients:

- 9 inches store bought pie dough
- ¾ cup of maple syrup
- ½ cup of pecans, finely chopped
- 2 eggs
- 2 tablespoons of cashew butter
- 2 tablespoons of brown sugar
- 1 tablespoon of butter
- ¾ teaspoon of vanilla extract
- ½ teaspoon of cinnamon
- 1/8 teaspoon of nutmeg powder

Directions:

1. Preheat the Airfryer on 356 F for 3 min.
2. Roll the pie dough on a floured surface then place it in a greased baking pan that fits in your Airfryer.
3. Melt the butter in a deep pan and cook in it the chopped pecans for 6 to 8 min the pour it in the pie shell.
4. Mix the remaining ingredients in a mixing bowl then pour it all over toasted pecans in the pie shell.
5. Garnish it the pie with some whole pecans then airfry it for 25 to 30 min.
6. Once the time is up, serve your pie with some ice cream and enjoy.

German Apple Cake

Serves: 4 to 6
Prep Time: 1 h
Ingredients:

- 4.5 ounces of purpose flour
- 3.5 ounces of brown sugar
- 2 cups of fresh apple, diced
- 1 egg
- 4 tablespoons of olive oil
- 1 tablespoon of fresh lemon juice
- 1 teaspoon of nutmeg powder
- 1 teaspoon of cinnamon
- ¾ teaspoon of vanilla extract
- ½ teaspoon of baking soda
- Salt

Directions:

1. Preheat the Airfryer on 356 F for 3 min.
2. Beat the vegetable oil with egg in a mixing bowl until they become pale.
3. Toss the apple with lemon juice and set it aside.
4. Mix the remaining ingredients in a mixing bowl then fold them into the egg and oil mix.
5. Fold the apples into the flour mix then press it into a greased baking pan.
6. Cover the cake with a piece of foil and pierce several holes in it.
7. Airfry the cake for 40 then remove the piece of foil and cook it for 5 min.
8. Serve your cake with some vanilla ice cream and enjoy.

Conclusion

Thank you again for going through this book! I really do hope you found the recipes as tasty and mouth watering as I did.

<u>You Might Also Love This Cookbook Below</u>

<u>Instant Pot Pressure Cooker Cookbook: 120 Delicious, Quick And Easy To Make Instant Pot Pressure Cooker Recipes You And Your Family Will Love So Much</u>

23420269R00094

Printed in Poland
by Amazon Fulfillment
Poland Sp. z o.o., Wrocław